Praise for *The Eterna*

The following comments came from readers and everyday moms:

"I have found a lot of encouragement from your book. Many days as I embark on the 'grind' of daily tasks, I often ask myself two questions—*What am I doing anyway?* and *Do my efforts really matter?* Your loving, wise counsel has helped me to reestablish a purpose, God's purpose, for raising these two precious gifts from God."

"I have been feeling very overwhelmed lately as a full-time mother and working full-time as a registered nurse. I believe God led me to your book. I needed to hear those encouraging words."

"Sometimes as a mother of small children I feel used, abused, and unappreciated. Your book brought back into focus the 'big picture' of what an important role I play as mom in my kids' lives."

"I especially appreciated what you said about nurturing. It is truly a high calling. My mother wasn't there to meet my emotional needs. Your book is a mentor to me, and I will refer back to it often."

"I must tell you how much I'm enjoying your book. I bought it after an extremely grueling day with my boys (ages two and one), and I needed your encouragement. It is so hard. I know I'll make a big difference in their lives. It just feels extremely good to see it in print."

"I am a physician specializing in internal medicine, formerly in active private practice. I now have five children, but I am committed to staying home while my children are small. This book provides a hearty rationale for choosing to make nurturing motherhood top priority as well as practical encouragement for mothers in a variety of situations. Childhood is fleeting. Linda Weber's book can help us make the most of it."

"I will never look at the job of motherhood in the same way."

"As a mother of three small children, it's easy to get lost in diapers, runny noses, and dirty dishes, but your book helped me to refocus. Thank you!"

"What an inspiration you were to me and my decision to stay home with our child and delay returning to our veterinary practice."

"Your book came to me just at a time when I was feeling overwhelmed, run-down, and stuck in a *why do I even bother, because nothing I do makes a difference anyway and*

I don't do any one thing really good attitude. You put me back into focus, reminding me that my calling to be the best wife and mom I can be is important! I once again feel very fulfilled and at peace."

"With my husband being a pastor in a small church, an extra income could come in handy, but the Lord has always provided our needs and given us the opportunity to raise our children at home. I thank you for providing a book to give moms an encouraging word!"

Being a mom of "littles" can be very challenging, but Linda shows us how important this time is. *The Eternal Mark of a Mom* helps guide us through this process of raising confident and strong children in a world of chaos and evil.

LISA ROBERTSON
Coauthor of *A New Season* and *The Women of Duck Commander*

From the day I met Linda Weber over 45 years ago, I witnessed her focus and intentionality as a mother. I know few people who have given more thought to motherhood than Linda has. *The Eternal Mark of a Mom* overflows with insights and wise advice. It offers truths and tools, principles and practices that will bring much-needed hope and help to moms.

RANDY ALCORN
Author of *Heaven, The Treasure Principle,* and *If God Is Good*

Being a mom of four strong-willed boys, I would have loved having Linda's book to help guide me. If you watched *Duck Dynasty*, you know I had my work cut out for me!

KAY ROBERTSON
Matriarch of the Robertson family from the hit show *Duck Dynasty*

It's said that women are uniquely built for nurturing children. Some do this in other ways besides mothering, but more than ever before mothers need to see that their contribution of raising up the next generation is invaluable. Linda Weber's words are worthy of attention and adherence.

JUDY TAYLOR
Mother of four, pastor's wife for 46 years, speaker for FamilyLife Weekend to Remember for 23 years

Having been a pediatrician for over 30 years, I see the need every day for moms to get guidance in parenting. This book will inspire married and single moms of all stages to do their best for their children. Our whole society could benefit from the words of wisdom and experience that Linda Weber has to offer us.

JO ANNE NIELSON, MD

THE ETERNAL MARK OF A MOM

THE ETERNAL MARK
OF A
mom

SHAPING THE WORLD THROUGH
THE HEART OF YOUR CHILD

LINDA WEBER

TYNDALE HOUSE PUBLISHERS, INC.
CAROL STREAM, ILLINOIS

FOCUS ON THE FAMILY® | FOCUS ON PARENTING™

For information about special discounts for bulk purchases, please contact Tyndale House Publishers at csresponse@tyndale.com, or call 1-800-323-9400.

Library of Congress Cataloging-in-Publication Data can be found at www.loc.gov.

ISBN 978-1-58997-967-3

Printed in the United States of America

25	24	23	22	21	20	19
7	6	5	4	3	2	1

I dedicate this to all the mothers out there who will read this book and benefit from its principles. May you indeed renew your awareness of the difference you can make in positively influencing the world. May you walk away with more confidence and be better equipped to influence future generations. You are heroes for the work you do. God bless each of you.

Table of Contents

Introduction

Mom, you have a life-changing mission. On some days, when you're deep in diapers or driving kids around and barely have a minute to text someone, you might wonder about that mission.

What was it again? And how do you accomplish it? Is there a motherhood GPS that can keep you moving in the right direction?

Yes, there is! This book is your GPS. It will remind you that the special role you play in your child's life is powerful, influential, important, and irreplaceable. The value of a conscientious, nurturing mother cannot be overstated.

She crafts the psyches of her little children in so many ways: She helps them develop a sense of security that will give them lifelong strength; she directs a child who tends to have a negative view of life to see instead through eyes of gratefulness and optimism; she protects her children's hearts and spirits.

With intelligence, she notices what's missing in her

children's worlds and steers them away from life's minefields and harmful pursuits. She skillfully guides her children so they can develop their individual talents and capitalize on the strengths of their natures. She prepares them to be launched into the world, ready to tackle any life assignment.

If you want influence, Mom, you've got it!

During your kids' vulnerable and moldable childhood years, you possess the power to prepare them for a complex world. With determination and skill, you run a business plan, if you will, with a goal of countering undesirable influences that have crept into our society and could lead your children in the wrong direction.

The work of a nurturing mother is essential and noble. Mom, I esteem you for the perseverance you display as you complete thousands of tasks each day to ensure the positive development of your children.

It is critical that you learn to feel good about who you are and what you do. You are not expendable. Your influence marks the world forever and leaves an important legacy. You should feel terrific about that. As you read the following pages, may you catch your value in a new and powerful way.

My purpose here is for you to come to believe anew that you're invaluable, and to raise your effectiveness to an all-time high. Mom, you leave an eternal mark on your children. As you shape their hearts, you shape the world.

CHAPTER I

DO WELL-ADJUSTED KIDS JUST HAPPEN?

As a mom, you've probably given deeply of yourself to your children—physically, emotionally, mentally, and spiritually. On hard days, you may sometimes wonder if it's all worth it, whether what you do day in and day out really matters in your child's life.

I'm here to tell you that everything you do as a mom is definitely worth it. And your role as a mother *does* matter—immensely!

Consider this Facebook post I came upon that took my breath away. I hope this post will motivate you to never give up and to realize that your behind-the-scenes work as a mother changes many lives for the good.

There once was a young boy who had potential, but he did not know it. However . . . the boy had a mother, who was always active and on alert. Her work would soon help him see the potential he possessed. It seemed as though she never slept. She was always awake when he awoke and worked hard far after he fell asleep.

Every time the boy's heart hurt, his mother was there to fill him with comfort and confidence. Every time there was danger, she scared off his aggressors. Every time the boy was sick, she cared for him. Every time he had the flu and vomited, she was right there rubbing his back, telling him it would soon pass.

Every night, and through the day, she would sing with him and taught him to be joyful despite life's circumstances. She constantly made him food, washed his clothes, cleaned up his messes, and navigated his dangerous and adventurous world to keep him safe. She not only tolerated his constant noise and activity that annoyed everyone else, but she also loved it.

He could tell she loved him. She put her life and desires on hold for his. With each act of love, even those the boy didn't understand at his young age, it strengthened his young heart and gave him courage and peace that would last a lifetime. When the boy became a man, he realized that his mother's tireless, selfless acts were responsible for everything he had, and all that he knew, every outlook he had, and the fun he always encountered.

When life became difficult for the young man as he grew, he knew he could not only make it through it but he could also come out on top, with joy and having learned something, because he remembered his mom's commitment as she tackled countless unknown obstacles for him. When the boy's obstacles came, he could hear a voice whispering encouragement, and he could feel his mom's hands on his back. He knew the difficult times would pass, and he would sing songs of God's providence that his mom taught him, as he rolled up his sleeves to be like her.

Mom, thank you. Linda Weber, there is no one like you. I do not deserve your love. But I am so grateful for it. Thank you for never giving up on me. Thank you for giving up your life to make mine. I love you, Mom!

That Facebook post was written by my son Ryan, and it blew me away! What he wrote so graciously shows the difference we moms make in our children's lives. I hope this post will help you feel the power of your hard work, moms. You do make an impact.

I know that a lot is expected of moms today. I want to say things were better for my mother. I suppose they were in a way. Being a mom was considered a full-time effort back then. No one chided, "Lean in to your career. Get out in the world and make a difference." She was never challenged to opt for a different focus. In her generation, if you were a mom, that's just who you were, first and foremost. Anything else was extra and secondary, even though she did have to work to keep us alive.

On the other hand, things were a lot harder for Mom. She had three children to raise and an angry, abusive husband to contend with. Eventually, my father abandoned us, which tells that story very mildly. He should have been in jail. This type of home situation could have caused many children to have major life problems. Instead, my siblings and I are a redemption story, praise God! (And you can be a redemption story too, if your circumstances weren't good.)

The responsibility of providing for the family always fell on Mom's shoulders. If we were going to eat, she had to work. And back in the 1960s, the job market for women was limited, both in choices and in pay. As I recall, she never made more than 200 dollars a month.

We lived in an apple orchard in a small structure built to house migrant workers. A couch sat against one wall of our tiny living room, and an old family upright piano covered the opposite wall. If I stood in the center of the room, I could reach out and touch both pieces at the same time.

Cold floors. No carpet. An oil stove for heat. The rent was 25 dollars a month. We used spare apple boxes for cupboards and dressers and covered them with old tea towels. We were allowed to collect the fallen apples and add to them the wild asparagus that grew here and there among the trees.

When the school year began, if we kids were lucky, we'd get to choose one pair of shoes to last us the year. Most of our clothes were hand-me-downs from other families, and they were limited. Occasionally, our grandmother would buy Easter dresses for my sister and me. When I got to high school, a friend's mother made clothes for me so I could look like everyone else.

What Mom lacked in wealth, however, she made up for in character. She was a devout Christian woman with a steady, thankful heart. She loved her God and read the Bible morning and night. She never did anything she feared was wrong, not even reusing a postage stamp that had been missed by the cancellation stamp. She trusted that God could handle anything we had to face, and she told us time and again, "God knows our need. He loves us. He'll provide."

The list of God's character traits, which she kept telling us about, was long. And those facts stay in our minds today: God will never leave us (He is always with us). God never makes mistakes. God is good because His way is perfect. God has the power to do all things. God never changes. God always keeps His promises. God is fair and will judge the wrong. He dispels confusion.

We knew we had this *big enough* God, so we could trust and follow Him with everything. We could do anything, and we didn't have to fear. As a result of Mom's strong faith in God, and since her God was our God, we were not reduced to becoming insecure people. What a gift. Because of this, my favorite Scripture verse is Matthew 19:26: "With man this is impossible, but with God all things are possible."

For all her sacrifices, for all she did without, Mom never made us feel it was our fault or that she was missing out on something. She never gave the impression she was "stuck" raising the three of us. She never gave those impressions because she never felt that way.

Mom was doing all she knew how to do in being a good mom. Working at a job outside the home was a necessary part of that, but we knew that she loved us. She didn't see any way to remove us from the traumas in the home—where do you take a family of four when you have no money? She was proud to be Mom to us. She invested her life in her children; she taught us about the hope we have in a strong God, and she did that with passion.

Was she perfect? No. Would it have been better if she had moved us to a women's shelter, away from the dad we had at home? Yes. Without shelters available in those years, she instead confided in her pastor about the abuse, but nothing ever transpired to move us all out of there.

We got by, but it wasn't easy. Even so, Mom kept a positive attitude while she focused on the *heart* and *spirit*. That's what she developed in us, and that need is still important for today—inner strength to face all the battles around.

Because she had a focus, because she knew one thing was more important than anything else, she has three successful, well-adjusted children who adore her. Her son, Bruce, is a pastor. Her two daughters, Judy and myself, married pastors.

And all of us raised our children with the same passion and focus Mom showed when we were young.

Well-adjusted children are shaped through hard work, incredible insights, and a large portion of unselfish giving of ourselves. (Glory in any field comes with sacrifice.) As with anything in life, however, there are no guarantees. Children become adults, and God made them with a will of their own. But this is your chance to do all you can to shape your child.

Despite any overwhelming circumstances you find yourself in, Mom, your chosen optimism and unwavering positive outlook will make huge differences in the life of your child.

Let's consider how a mother of six, while leading an overwhelmed life, would teach her children that being happy wasn't dependent on their circumstances.[1] And years later, her sons reflected on this principle and said, "She showed us that optimism is a courageous choice you can make every day, especially in the face of adversity."[2]

You see, this mom and dad were in a near-death car accident when the kids were little. Mom survived with only a few broken bones, but the father lost the use of his right hand. Through the stress and frustration that the father felt, he developed a harsh temper. Life was not perfect, but Mom still believed that "life was *good*."[3] Because of this, the kids did not develop a victim mentality.

Each night at the dinner table, this mom said to her children, "Tell me something good that happened today." Her sons Bert and John Jacobs were so influenced by their mom's emphasis on being a master of attitude and gratitude that they started making and selling "Life Is Good" T-shirts, which has developed into a $100 million clothing empire. It was their mother who planted that seed.[4] Now you and I may not inspire huge business ventures, but our influence is powerful and substantial.

Moms, we need to see mothering—developing a child's heart and spirit—as the main thing, the central focus of our efforts. And as the German proverb says, "The main thing is that the main thing always remains the main thing."

Well-adjusted kids come from families in which mothering is seen as a complex, beautiful challenge worthy of everything a mom can give to it. Mothering shapes lives and attitudes, one way or the other.

That's not to say you have to stay home all the time to be a decent mother. My mom worked at outside jobs. She had to. Today, more moms than ever have to fit work into their schedules. In fact, in 2017, the labor force participation rate of mothers with children under six years old was 65.1 percent.[5]

My mom understood the importance of giving her best efforts to what was most important—her children. Despite all the demands on a working mom in the 1960s, she understood the need to be there during the rehearsals of life—the learning stages of our youth—so that when the curtain went up for each of us, we could perform well. That meant setting the stage by developing our character and confidence. Though Mom didn't give us a high standard of living, she gave us a high standard of life. It didn't matter how many rooms our little migrant worker's house had. What mattered was how our hearts and spirits were developed in those rooms.

These days, moms need to be increasingly astute. Raising children in a rapidly changing culture presents new challenges, of which you are undoubtedly well aware: rampant teen suicide, sex trafficking, sexting, an increasingly genderless society, transgender/transition living, social media bullying, same-sex marriage, legalized marijuana, the easy availability of drugs, school shootings by troubled kids, pornography—this tragic list could go on and on.

One nice girl I knew from a diligent, caring home actually crawled into her parents' bedroom while they were asleep to retrieve her phone—her parents kept it under their bed in an effort to keep her safe. This girl wanted to interact with a guy she had met online, but the parents woke up and stopped that advance. The mom messaged the guy and later called him, telling him to never contact her daughter again or there would be serious consequences for him.

Yes, a lot *is* expected of moms today. The truth is, motherhood can't be discounted. It can't be devalued. And it can't be approached casually. If we want to do well at mothering, we're going to have to study, which you are seeking to do here.

Conscientious mothers nurture a healthy self-esteem and emotional security in their kids; their children enjoy self-confidence and a sense of direction for their lives.

Doesn't it just make sense to give mothering your best

efforts? Trying to raise well-adjusted kids requires an investment of your life in theirs—the *best* of your life, not the leftovers. It takes lots of time, lots of energy, lots of commitment, lots of wisdom.

Mom, if you don't do it, who will? If this isn't all-important, next to the nurturing of your marriage, what is? The challenge is yours. Will your family enjoy the positive results of your efforts?

"I need my shortsighted vision of motherhood corrected with an eternal perspective," writes Gloria Furman, mama of four and author of *Missional Motherhood: The Everyday Ministry of Motherhood in the Grand Plan of God.* "Otherwise I will not keep my gaze fixed on the horizon of eternity."[6]

If you haven't done it before, won't you commit yourself right now to making the main thing the main thing? What better legacy could you leave to your children than your full investment in their growing-up years?

If you've already made that nurturing commitment, take pride in your decision. Affirm it. Motherhood is the greatest cause you could follow, and you've given yourself to it. Now do all you can to live out that decision with excellence!

CHAPTER 2

IS THERE LIGHT AT THE END OF THIS TUNNEL?

FINALLY, a night out of the house. No laundry. No demands. Just some relaxation, some time for me.

Then came the emergency phone call.

"Mom, you gotta come home. Ryan climbed into the grandfather clock, and it fell over, and the clock's all over the floor, and Ryan's crying."

That kid! My clock! My night out! Good grief, Lord!

Ryan was always into everything. Can't you just imagine this little kid exploring the house, looking for a place to hide? He found it in the antique grandfather clock. The *beautiful* clock we'd brought back from Germany after a tour in the Army. *My* clock. My pride and joy. One of the few things of grace and beauty in a struggling young family's home furnished mostly in early in-law.

Now, as Ryan boosted himself into the cabinet to hide behind the pendulum, the whole thing had come crashing down.

Will there ever be any light at the end of this tunnel?

That wasn't the first time the question had crossed my mind. In fact, there were lots of those times when the boys were little. My husband, Stu, was in seminary. Money was tight, and luxuries were nonexistent. We were new in town and didn't know anyone in our neighborhood. There was absolutely no money for babysitters, and I rarely got any help with the kids from Stu, who was overwhelmed with attending classes, studying, and holding down two jobs. Talk about the housebound mama! We barely had enough for the essentials. I took care of the boys, cooked, washed, and did the unending housework.

I once read that doing housework was like stringing beads with no knot at the end. I felt as if my whole life were stringing beads.

Even later, during the boys' high-school years, there were times when motherhood took all I had. Once when Stu was in Africa on a mission trip, I got a call late at night from two of my three boys. Hearing kids laughing in the background, I assumed everybody was having a good time.

"So what have you been doing tonight?" I asked.

Their response: "We wrecked the car."

I figured this was a joke, so I repeated my question three

times, but they kept giving me the same answer. It turns out that on an icy road at a hairpin curve, they crashed the car into a big tree and totaled the car. Fortunately, the five kids inside weren't hurt.

And I can't forget the time when two of the boys were returning at 1:00 a.m. from a job they had some miles away. Somehow a policeman mistook their car for one belonging to a dangerous criminal who had fired a shot through a lady's window in the neighborhood. Not only were my boys and their friend stopped, but they were also thrown to the ground with a gun pointed closely to their heads. Needless to say, there was some emotional trauma, but it turned out okay.

I can look back now and laugh as I see it all in perspective, but there were times when I felt motherhood was sapping everything from me. My time wasn't my own, my body wasn't my own, demands were placed on me every waking hour, and often my sleep was sacrificed. And even my love for playing tennis was put on an 11-year hold.

<hr />

Is there light at the end of this tunnel?

In the early days, God answered my question.

One cold morning as we headed for church, one of the babies burped up his breakfast all over my only coat. The stain and stench permeated it, so there was no coat for now. I took it to the cleaners the next day, where they actually ruined it and wouldn't take responsibility. They told me the coat had a manufacturing defect and then suggested I return it to the store.

But we were living in Oregon, and I had purchased the coat when we were stationed in Germany. I had received some money for my birthday and wanted to buy a new Bible, but now I needed a coat! How discouraging.

Nevertheless, God provided. A store owner graciously offered me a coat for a largely discounted amount. And to the penny, I ended up with a new coat *and* the Bible I wanted with what little money I had! God's provision was a light-in-the-tunnel experience for me.

What would happen if I were in the same situation today? Some people would tell me, "Well, it's obvious you need to go to work. Your whole family would be better off if you have more income. And you need to do it for you, too. You don't have to settle for being a maid and a bottle washer. Everyone needs fulfillment. Get a job—you've got lots of potential. The boys will be fine. Kids are resilient. In fact, it will be good for them."

We really did need the money, but my husband and I knew our children needed the stability and security of having me at home. It was our choice.

As moms, we have so many decisions to make as we try to give our kids the best guidance in life and also care for ourselves. Many women have extensive educational backgrounds and are extremely talented. They can excel at their vocations. So, what to do? We must realize that there are seasons of life when we major in one thing while minoring in others. After one season comes another, and the focus changes. Deciding how we arrange our 24-hour days throughout life is not easy.

One friend of mine was an excellent teacher. I remember when she had her first baby. She was so excited, so enthusiastic about staying home with her child. But her principal at school and her fellow teachers just wouldn't give up. She *couldn't* waste all that talent and *just* stay home. She *needed* to go back to work. It was the "right" thing to do, they said.

In times like that, you need to be able to look down the road beyond today's obstacles and see your goal. (My friend did and resisted the pressure to return to work.) You need perspective to make those critical choices. You need to tell yourself, *This is important. It's not a waste of my life or talents. The future of these kids depends on me now.*

That's what I did, and it has made a difference. My boys have written me numerous notes of thanks over the years for majoring in mothering instead of being distracted by other pursuits. They noticed. It had an impact that they continue to appreciate. If we're not willing to empty ourselves to fill up our children, who will be?

My husband would jokingly say that after the boys left home, so did we! In this new season of life, I have pursued career opportunities and other interests that I didn't when my boys were home. I could have explored those things earlier, but I wasn't willing to expend my energy in that way. There were so many nuances of my boys' emotional needs that could not be crafted if I were heavily distracted with too many other interests. One parent needs to be closely tuned in to the children. Something has to give when there are too many responsibilities, and we don't want it to be the security of our kids' hearts.

I received a desperate phone call one day from my friend Kay, who was in over her head with a toddler and an infant. Kay is a capable, intelligent woman, a trained psychologist. But she wasn't feeling very capable then. In fact, she was ready to throw in the towel. This mothering business was for the birds, she said. It had been a long way from the halls of academia to the changing table, and at the moment it seemed like the wrong direction.

She pleaded incompetence. She begged for escape. She felt trapped, breathless. The endless clutter was closing in on her, and she was ready to run.

"I'm tired all the time," she said. "I can't get on top of anything. These kids have insatiable needs and demands. And even they don't know why they're crying."

Sound familiar?

By her own admission, Kay was "freaking out." (Psychologists can be so clinical.) The two-year-old seemed bent on destroying everything in his path, the baby never stopped screaming . . . and then there was that forever need to be changing another diaper.

"Help!" she begged.

That week, I'd received letters from our two older boys,

who were away in college. I read the letters to her. They told how thankful they were for me, how much they were coming to realize and appreciate all my sacrifices, my taxi service, and my time spent with them.

By the time I finished reading the letters, Kay was crying— not because she couldn't take it anymore, but because some of her perspective had been restored. She decided to abandon her present trend of feeling like a victim. She had seen beyond the day's obstacles to her goals for tomorrow.

While my kids were in school, I began to take on part-time jobs. One was working special sales at a big department store. As the shoppers stampeded into the aisles as the doors opened, I was reminded of how often I felt stampeded by the demands of mothering little ones. And Kay had been caught up in this too, riding herd on the "wild years" when the investment is just being made, long before you begin to enjoy any of the dividends.

In those times, you need reminders of "the main thing." You need a vision to focus upon. You need to know, even though it may not look as if your efforts are bearing fruit, that they will pay off one day, and that the chances are excellent that they will provide great satisfaction. Everything you do has its impact.

For instance, all three of our sons love sports—all sports. About the time they reached junior-high age, I took each of them to the local tennis courts to teach them the game. I spent hour after hour hitting the ball, returning volleys, and helping them develop a serve. We'd keep at it until we were both exhausted. I don't know which was harder, hitting all the balls or dishing out all the encouragement to keep them going.

In that junior-high season, one of my guys had a hard time. He'd miss the ball, make mistakes, and then get down on himself. His racket would drop, his head would hang, and his shoulders would droop.

"Come on," I'd say, "try it again. You'll get it." Day after day, I was his cheerleader. What a struggle! I thought I'd collapse. *Could this possibly ever be worth all the hassle?* I sometimes wondered—I was emotionally exhausted.

Then his game began to click. He improved steadily. As Kent and Blake entered high school, they played as doubles partners on the school team together and became district champions besting nine large high schools. After Kent graduated, Blake found another partner, and they repeated the championship.

Later, both boys went on to play competitively in college. Kent was nationally ranked and was an all-American and a national scholar/athlete. Blake has since coached a high-school team into state competition, winning significant tournaments himself, and Kent was a tennis pro for a while. Ryan, our youngest, was a varsity letterman on his high-school team for four years, was named most valuable player time and again, and has coached many different sports for his four kids.

Was the effort worth it? The boys think so. The tennis scholarships allowed them to travel to several foreign countries, something we could never have provided. Kent's earnings as tennis pro helped pay for graduate school.

In addition to developing character, my sons learned perseverance, self-discipline, and how to win and lose gracefully—all such good life lessons. What positive results! They felt good about themselves. They had the satisfaction and pleasure of their accomplishments, and they continue to have confidence in life. So much started by taking the time to hit the ball, build them up, hit the ball again, and build them up again.

Things would have been different had I given in to the stampede of demands and decided other things were more important than to work with them.

Mom, don't underestimate your impact. Abraham Lincoln once said he considered his mother to be the person chiefly responsible for all he was or ever hoped to become.[1] She was just a poor, simple country mother. But she taught him about sacrifice. She taught him to read. And she gave him a healthy self-image that sustained him through a lifetime of challenges, disappointments, and defeats. That's quite a legacy!

Thomas Edison's mother taught him at home after she learned his teachers considered him to have inferior ability. "My mother was the making of me," he said later in life. "She was so true, so sure of me; and I felt that I had someone to live for, someone I must not disappoint."[2]

You don't have to be someone of note to make a note-worthy impact on someone else's life. Just be faithful in your efforts, keep focused on the main thing, and watch what happens. History is written by little people in little places doing what they should.

There are times we try to defy the reality of 24 hours in a day, when we take on more and more responsibilities and tasks than are physically possible to do well. Because we're so smart, we can give many reasons why we need to do *everything*. We'll utter the words "I just have to."

Yet if we run ourselves into the ground, nobody wins. If we face reality, we know we need to carefully prioritize every day and every season so we do justice to ourselves, our families, and the jobs we take on. Most of us don't like this reality.

If you are in a dark season, read on to find encouragement. There is light at the end of the tunnel. You bet there is! Keep believing. Keep focusing. Come on, hit the ball, and build up those kids.

CHAPTER 3

DID YOU SAY *JUST* A MOTHER?

CHESKA SAMACO dreams of being a housewife and mother. Unfortunately in today's world, a young woman who would like to raise children to be good people is not understood.

Cheska blogged in 2016 about this dilemma:

> A few weeks back, a friend asked me if I wanted to work for the government, to which I responded "no." He asked, "Oh, so you want to go corporate?" I said, "not really." "What do you want to be then?" he said. And I replied, "I want to be a housewife—a mother."
>
> And I was baffled (still am) about his response to my proud answer. His first response was "Seriously?"

with that awful tone of disgust. And then he followed this up with possibly the worst question I have ever been asked, *"Don't you want to contribute to society?"* And ever since that moment, I realized how mistaken and shallow people could be in the way they define and measure the intangibles of the world.[1]

Mom, don't let society's lack of respect for your work get you down. Don't let anyone convince you it's not worth doing. And please remember, the issue isn't about having a job outside the home. My mother did, and after my boys reached a certain age, I did too. The problem is that people think you *need* a job to be a whole person—to use your brain or to meaningfully contribute to the world.

Cheska could have told her friend that moms are the developers of national security and the directors of health, education, and welfare. She could have said a mom can be the secretary of the treasury, the head of public affairs, and the chairman of the house rules committee.

If someone says, "Don't you want to contribute to society?" you can respond this way: "I'm responsible for building my kids' sense of emotional security. I'm responsible for teaching my kids everything from how to chew food to how to drive a car, and I also prevent psychological, physical, and spiritual disasters on a regular basis. By the way, what do *you* contribute to society?"

To put it another way, the issue is not whether there's an

outside job in your schedule, but rather what's most important in your schedule. Be honest with yourself as you look at your schedule. If you conclude that mothering has become secondary in your life, you're going to have to expect secondary results.

If you choose to work outside the home, make sure you have your priorities in focus. And do so understanding just how much you're committing yourself to. Most people don't realize all a mother is called upon to do. The list below refers merely to the thousands of *physical* things we do, but you can be sure that this type of care *does* send messages of love and security to children.

Many years ago, a mom wrote this list and then sent this letter to a national columnist:

> I am so tired of all those ignorant people who
> come up to my husband and ask him if his wife
> has a full-time job or is she "just a housewife."
> Please print this letter and shed some light on this
> sorely undervalued occupation. Thank you. . . .
> Here is my job description: I am a wife, mother,
> friend, confidant, personal adviser, lover, referee,
> peacemaker, housekeeper, laundress, chauffeur,
> interior decorator, gardener, painter, wallpaperer,
> dog groomer, veterinarian, manicurist, barber,
> seamstress, appointment manager, financial planner,
> bookkeeper, money manager, personal secretary,
> teacher, disciplinarian, entertainer, psychoanalyst,

nurse, diagnostician, public relations expert, dietitian and nutritionist, baker, chef, fashion coordinator and letter writer for both sides of the family.

I am also a travel agent, speech therapist, plumber and automobile maintenance and repair expert. During the course of my day I am supposed to be cheerful, look radiant and jump in the sack on a moment's notice. . . .

I took time out of my busy day to write this letter . . . because there are still ignorant people who believe that a housewife is nothing more than a baby-sitter who sits on her behind all day and looks at soap operas.

If I could afford to pay someone to do all the things that I do, I would be delighted to go back to working an eight-hour day with an hour for lunch and two 15-minute breaks.

What do I get out of my job in the absence of a salary? Joy, happiness, hugs, kisses, smiles, love, self-respect and pride in knowing that I have done a full day's work to ensure the physical and emotional well-being of those I love.

Now if you still want to classify me as just a housewife, go ahead.[2]

You can identify with her, can't you? I love to read her letter to women when I speak on mothering. Invariably, that mom's message brings great applause. Yes, the job entails menial busywork, but it also requires heart connection work—work that meets the needs of children's souls and builds within them a sense of security that will last a lifetime.

Developer of Security

Helping a child build a sense of security is just one aspect of a mom's job, but it's an important one. Emotional security gives us feelings of safety and confidence. The psychological definition of *security* is having "feelings of basic safety, assurance, and independence from alarm." A sense of security is "engendered by such conditions as a comforting, approving support system of family and friends; progression of age-appropriate abilities and competencies; and occurrences that boost ego sturdiness."[3] As moms, we can help our children develop emotional security and emotional maturity.

William Menninger, cofounder of the Menninger Clinic (ranked as one of the nation's best hospitals for psychiatric treatment), offered these seven criteria of emotional maturity:

1. The ability to deal constructively with reality
2. The capacity to adapt to change
3. A relative freedom from symptoms that are produced by tensions and anxieties
4. The capacity to find more satisfaction in giving than receiving
5. The capacity to relate to other people in a consistent manner with mutual satisfaction and helpfulness

6. The capacity to sublimate, to direct one's instinctive hostile energy into creative and constructive outlets
7. The capacity to love[4]

Don't we want our children to have those qualities?

In *Raising an Emotionally Intelligent Child*, psychologist John Gottman writes, "Researchers have found that even more than IQ, your emotional awareness and ability to handle feelings will determine your success and happiness in all walks of life, including family relationships."[5]

Other experts tell us that a securely attached child is a child who feels emotionally secure because of a good attachment, or a good emotional bond, with the mother.

A mom's job description includes developing security in her child and preventing insecurity from dictating her child's every decision. Maureen Healy, child development expert and author of *Growing Happy Kids*, sees what happens when security is missing in the lives of children.

"Many of my child clients had absentee parents, and this was a major cause of low self-confidence. Such children grow up yearning to feel loved and valuable, while often looking for it in all the wrong places (for example, making perfect grades to feel valuable or joining a 'gang' to gain a sense of belonging)."[6]

William Sears and Martha Sears, a doctor and nurse who authored *The Discipline Book*, also write about how emotional security can affect a child: "A child who feels right acts right. . . . The growing person with a positive self-image is easier to discipline. She thinks of herself as a worthwhile person, and so she behaves in a worthwhile way. . . . The child who doesn't feel right doesn't act right."[7]

So many "mom decisions" can communicate approval, appreciation, acceptance, and importance to a child. Are you continually showing your children that you care? Doing so develops security and multiplies good and positive behaviors.

Just a mom? Hardly.

But you don't have to do the challenging job alone, Mom. You can gain strength from the Lord, the Creator of all human beings, the One who can give you instruction and help you make things happen. As you provide a secure environment for your children, you can also teach them to be secure in the Lord. Remember what Proverbs 14:26 says: "In the fear of the LORD one has strong confidence."

So you see, moms have a strong calling to provide healthy conditions that will influence their children for a lifetime. The job is so much more than making peanut butter sandwiches and changing diapers. Let's avoid the trap of the condescending title "Just a mother." Let's demonstrate motherhood to be the honorable position God intends.

If you think about all that moms are supposed to do to launch their kids safely into this world, you may feel as I used to feel: as if you're trying to launch a spaceflight. The atmosphere your kids are destined for seems no less dangerous, and the thousands of details that need attention before liftoff seem as important as any NASA research, training, or construction project. Too much is at stake to get sloppy or neglect any responsibilities.

Moms, remember that every mother is a working mother. Can we be too prepared as mothers, know too much? Can we possibly be overqualified? As essential partners in marriage or in any business, the more expertise we bring, the more time and diligence we dedicate to the task at hand, the better return we receive.

But what if your time and energy are already maxed out by demands outside your home? How will your child's inner needs be met—even be recognized? The more needs that go unmet, the more problems will arise. If a mother's life gets too crowded with demands, some things will be left undone. Isn't it better to do some careful evaluating now and make the choices of what gets the attention and what is put aside? Without our making conscious choices, things happen by default, and the urgent things may get more attention than the important.

Every family is different. Every set of circumstances is unique. Just how you go about dividing responsibilities with your husband or chores among your children is up to you. The point is for you to ensure that your family is cared for in a healthy, balanced manner.

Will we mothers be fully appreciated for all our efforts? For now, probably not.

If you need instant gratification for your mothering, you might become disappointed. But over the years, you'll receive more appreciation than you can imagine. Don't focus on today's lack of appreciation. Self-sacrifice has always been a trait of great mothers. For now, you may just have to remind yourself of the importance of your role and the importance of the ones you love who are at stake. Hopefully this book can remind you of this importance, and someday, your family will show their full appreciation.

You will experience times that give you a boost. One day my son Blake was buying a Mother's Day gift for me. The store salesperson asked if Mom had any Precious Moments, referring to the figurine series. Blake answered, "Yes, my mom and I have had lots of precious moments."

Don't feel as if you have to check your brains at the door, either. I've used all my abilities to undergird my family. Someday, in some way, you'll have to use all of yours.

Just a mother? Mothers must be prepared for anything.

My sister, Judy, and her husband, Rick, took their clan out for breakfast one Saturday morning at a camp where Rick worked. Kyle was five, Bryan was three, Eric was two, and within a couple of months, a fourth child was due. After breakfast, Judy and the kids returned home to get ready for a party and Rick left for work.

While Judy wrapped a package for the party, the boys asked to go outside to play. "Sure," she told them. They played outside all the time, and she wouldn't be long with her project. For some reason, the boys wandered farther from the house than ever before—all the way to a nearby pond. One at a time, they tried to jump over a little dam holding back runoff from a recent rainstorm. Kyle made it. Bryan made it. But Eric, the littlest, didn't make it and fell into deep water. Big brother Kyle jumped in to save him. Kyle made it to Eric's still body, tried to pull on him, and yelled to Bryan, "He's too heavy! Go get Mom!" Soon Kyle and Eric both disappeared under the muddy water.

By this time, Judy had finished wrapping the present and called to the boys. When they didn't respond, she went looking for them. She hurried toward the pond, and there she found Bryan in shock, unable to say much except that the other two were "dying in the water." Judy, seven months pregnant, scoured the edges of the pond and then jumped into the water, searching frantically along the muddy bottom for the boys. As she got stuck and then pulled herself from the weeds that edged the pond, she looked toward heaven and prayed loudly, "Please don't take both!"

Just as she was looking down, Eric surfaced out in the middle of the pond. She swam out to him, pulled him from the water, and began CPR on her motionless son, who was blue and had no heartbeat. Fortunately, Judy was skilled in the lifesaving procedure and was able to revive him after eight minutes.

Meanwhile, Kyle never surfaced. Judy knew if Eric were to live, she needed quick medical help at a hospital. Probably the hardest assignment of her life was driving away with Eric on that traumatic ride to town. Having to leave Kyle unseen and not retrieved, so Eric could receive help to live, was a horrible experience. Kyle was lodged under the water and had drowned.

Although Eric was submerged under the cold water for

five or more minutes, he lived and didn't suffer any brain damage. He is now an incredible young man and is flourishing in life. Judy was called to do an ultimate task as a mom that day: to save her child. It's sad that her valiant efforts were overshadowed by the terrible loss. She did everything possible and made a difference. She saved a life.[8]

That is an extreme example, but stories help us remember important points. I want to leave you with this thought: I hope you'll never be called to save your child's life like Judy, but you *are* called upon to shape your children's lives. And you know what? In the long run, shaping your child's life *is* saving it. It's a wicked world out there, and you make a difference in keeping your children from disasters of all kinds.

Did you say you were "just a mother"? Oh no, my dear, you're not. You're so much more! (For an extensive look at all the things that may demand your attention, please refer to the appendix, "What in the World Does Mom Do All Day?")

CHAPTER 4

CAN WE REALLY MAKE A DIFFERENCE?

THE NEWSPAPER ARTICLE said she was a beautiful girl, a high-school student, and an exceptional basketball player. She came from a good home, and life was promising. We'll call her Jenny. Jenny lived for basketball—until her injury. Being sidelined for part of the season seemed almost unbearable. Learning she would never play again was crushing. The family was devastated.

To somehow make up for her loss, her parents, who had both been poor when they were growing up, decided to give Jenny what they had lacked—things. And because of their acquired wealth, they gave her many extravagant items.

Clothes overflowed her closet. Cars filled the driveway.

A private airplane took them wherever they wanted. They even bought a hot air balloon. Jenny lacked nothing, her parents thought.

Surely this would dispel her disappointment. But, instead of rising above the situation, Jenny fell into depression. She felt unimportant. Her self-esteem collapsed. Her temper tantrums became unmanageable.

One Sunday morning, Jenny's mother went to Jenny's bedroom to wake her for breakfast. The girl lay facedown. She was wearing her prom dress, her bare feet hanging over the end of the bed. Her mom reached down to massage a foot to wake her and found her skin was cold. Jenny had taken her life.

Jenny's mom said, "We did everything for this girl," in stunned disbelief. How could it have happened? She was young and pretty. She had wealth and a promising life ahead. What more could anyone have done?

How can we know if we're making a difference in our children's lives? What *will* make a real difference?

In a coloring book, it doesn't matter how simple or complex the drawings are; they always seem flat, lifeless, and two-dimensional. But when color is added, it brings life and dimension. Until color is added, the outlined characters merely exhibit potential. Color brings completion.

Kids are a lot like those outlined drawings. The houses they live in, the things they own—the bikes, balls, toys, or clothes—the schools they've attended, and the training they've received are only black boundary lines on a white background, if you will. If that's all there is, the figures remain flat, lifeless, two-dimensional. What may be missing are the colors of self-worth, spiritual and emotional security, self-image, and confidence.

Jenny had all the bold lines, but evidently the colors inside were too pale to sustain her. She hadn't grieved her loss to the point of healing. Her heart and soul had become sick. She lost hope in the midst of an abundance of things. Obviously, her parents had tried to help her overcome her disappointment, but from a distance, it appears as if more time were spent drawing new lines than bringing color to what was already there. By majoring in mothering, we can add the color to our kids' lives.

Dads understand lines, boundaries, and borders. They focus on goals like providing for their kids' sports equipment, orthodontic braces, or college tuition. Dads will give their lives for lines.

Moms, on the other hand, understand nuance, nurturing, and developing. Moms color in the blank spaces. With our more sensitive natures, we're more attuned to what hurts, what's wrong, what intimidates. With that understanding, provided we focus our attention on mothering and spend our best efforts on our kids, we can provide the color and shading that bring depth and dimension to their lives.

Maybe it was good that our family didn't have much money in the early years. Because we were on such a tight budget, I couldn't get distracted pursuing too many physical concerns—the things I could buy for the kids. Instead, my focus was on creating a comfortable, encouraging environ-ment to grow in, regardless of "bumps in the road." I was tuned in to how unique each son was. I saw their individual needs. The more I worked at understanding how each one ticked, the more I could help each grow, and the more suc-cess we enjoyed.

Kent is our firstborn, excelling at everything he touched. When working as a tennis pro for a season, he observed a world of folk who lived in wealth and luxury yet felt unloved, uncared for, and unfulfilled. Elaborate bold lines. But no color. He saw it and didn't want to live that way. We had tried to live life at home by coloring in the lines.

Blake received a letter one day from a friend saying that the thing that stood out most about him was that he obviously cared a lot more about people than things. How rewarding to see my son reproduce what had been planted at home. The color showed. Someone could see his depth.

Ryan, our third-born, is Mr. Wise, continually seeing where people are at and artistically building them up and coloring in their lines. He's been a coach for many years, and kids like being on his team because he colors them in with reinforcement. Many don't get that kind of attention at home.

My high-school Latin teacher always challenged us to "name six" whenever we tried to answer one of her ques-tions. She wanted six examples or reasons for every answer we gave. It was her way of making sure we understood all aspects of what we were talking about. Perhaps it would be good to "name six" for you in answering why your best efforts are needed and how your actions really can make an impact. There will be some overlap between the six, but I hope that by looking at these issues from various perspectives, you'll gain a fresh appreciation for the impact you can have.

1. Kids need to feel worthwhile and accepted.

We communicate acceptance to our children as we let them be who they are—as we, for example, let a four-year-old act like a four-year-old. Not expecting perfection or even advanced behavior says, "I accept you now, not only after you change or grow up." And such acceptance without conditions is essential to a healthy self-esteem.

Mom, even when there are grass stains, a broken window, spilled syrup, or stupid behavior, our proper attitude toward the inner person within our children nourishes the good feelings they need about being accepted.

When we focus on our kids in a positive way, helping them develop confidence, every aspect of their lives is affected. Being around for our kids during the day, being available, dispels loneliness. Smiles and hugs are comforting. Signs of approval encourage and strengthen. They create comfort zones. And being included in our activities makes our kids feel they're worthwhile.

Dr. Ray Guarendi has written lessons he learned from observing 100 of America's happiest families. He says,

> Making ourselves accessible to our children forges
> more than a durable family bond. It also provides

them with a sense of security. No matter what
life away from home deals them, no matter what
risks they take and lose, no matter what outside
supports they watch crumble beneath them, the
unquestionable presence of their parents remains.
The certainty that there is always a place to gather
and regroup will bolster a youngster's self-confidence
as he prepares for another run at the world. . . .
Nothing can more quietly and surely build a child's
self-confidence than knowing his parents will be
present and supportive, whenever, however.[1]

Guarendi goes on to say, "Attentive presence is a quiet way to say, 'I love you. You are most special in my life.'" He tells how easy it is to affirm a child's worth. We can simply look up from what we're doing and listen to a choppy version of a joke we heard years ago, showing interest and demonstrating our acceptance.[2]

In *Parents* magazine, Ellie Kahan quotes Dr. Barbara Berger, a child and adolescent therapist in New York, who says, "Self-esteem is a child's pride in himself. To have high self-esteem, a child must feel both lovable and capable. He must believe that he is worthwhile, has something to offer, and can handle himself and his environment."[3]

Writer Kahan goes on to say, "The degree to which a child feels lovable and capable affects every area of his life and future. It's an important factor in determining a child's ability to be creative, relate to others, and to achieve."[4]

When your children feel accepted and see you readily accept others, they'll accept others more easily. They'll feel confident to reach out. Since our boys grew up in a pastor's home, they were exposed to many guests, from missionaries and nationally known speakers to battered mothers and other people in crisis. Many of these people have lived with us for seasons. It's been fun to see how the boys have been influenced by our acceptance of them and others.

Blake, our second-born, has never met a stranger and is rarely intimidated. He has invited his college president and visiting international speakers to his roommate's house for burgers. He's looked up the addresses of famous athletes and stopped by to meet them and learn from them. He's found himself inside pro-basketball locker rooms with Michael Jordan and others and has photos to prove it. He's definitely enjoying life because he feels good about himself.

We've also noticed that making each of our sons feel accepted while growing up minimized the natural temptation to compare themselves to one another or to doubt themselves. From the beginning, they were built differently and had different interests and skills. But because they felt accepted within our home for who they were, they didn't feel the need to match up to or best one another.

Believe it or not, I've also found that how you accept your children will be reflected in how your children accept you. A friend's daughter works with high-school girls. Again and again, she sees girls pulling away from their parents when they leave the house. She told her mom, "I know why I didn't have that problem. You accepted me." And as a result, she can accept her mom as well.

In contrast, we can learn from a common thread in the lives of hardened criminals. The famous ones and the ones we read about almost daily or hear about in news reports are often folk who *weren't accepted* by their parents and were *not* encouraged to feel worthwhile. That speaks for itself.

2. Kids need to feel important.

Every time you make a choice regarding your kids, you send a message. You can't make it to a game? Your kids think it must not be important to you. Don't have time for the concert? It probably doesn't matter much to you.

Just the opposite happens when you do make the effort. How many times have you heard an adult talking about the impression made by a mom or dad who never missed a game, always came to the concerts, or always had *time*? Those are lasting impressions that will have a lifelong influence on who your kids become.

With our three boys, ball games were important. Stu and I sat through hundreds of tennis and soccer matches, as well as basketball and football games. In one season alone, we attended 82 basketball games. After our kids graduated from high school, I calculated that we attended a grand total of 1,800 games. Now we're enjoying our 10 grandchildren's many games.

How we spend our time, with or without our children,

speaks loudly and clearly. Every time we make a sacrifice, it's remembered.

One friend remembers how his mother sat up all night, patiently holding in place his two front teeth that his brother had dislodged rather unceremoniously while they were wrestling. When they were able to get to a dentist the next morning, they learned that if not for her loving attention, the teeth would have been permanently damaged. Instead, even after all these years, every morning when he looks in the mirror to brush his teeth, he has a renewed opportunity to remember his mother's love and devotion.

You never know exactly what will register with boys; mine remember French toast. For some reason, my making French toast for breakfast on game days using real French bread seemed like a sacrifice and spoke volumes to them. It has become a family memory.

Affirmation of any kind lingers long after the event. It fosters a sense of importance and self-confidence. It enhances healthy self-esteem and emotional security.

A neighbor of ours returned to teaching in an elementary school after an 11-year absence being a mom at home. "What's the biggest change you see after so many years away?" I asked. Without hesitation, she answered, "The emotional insecurity of the kids."

Many parents are so busy that the kids aren't sure where they fit in their parents' hectic schedules or lists of priorities. The pace, the demands, the trips to day care and other places can be overwhelming. Children need a haven, a quiet, safe, comfortable setting where they can make mistakes without ridicule, try without competition, enjoy a relaxed pace, get special attention, and experience boundaries.

Our area has a lot of nurseries where shrubs and trees are grown for landscaping. Each gardener has greenhouses where the cuttings are first planted and grown. The protected environment doesn't make the plants weak and unhealthy. Just the opposite. The gardener knows the young cuttings need the enclosed environment so they can grow strong root structures and get a healthy start. Then when they're placed out in the real world, they thrive.

Too many children today are struggling with emotional insecurity because their parents don't realize how important that safe haven is. "Put them in day care," many people say. "It'll be good for them. Those folks are trained. It'll give the kids a head start in school."

Day care isn't so much the problem as is expecting day care to do the job of coloring in the lines of our kids' lives so they develop feelings of acceptance, importance, and self-esteem. It's expecting that the root structure will just grow automatically so they'll be strong and thrive in the real world.

Whenever there are strangers and peers, there will be competition—for recognition, for approval, for acceptance, for importance. And there will be winners and losers. Every kid needs to begin in a setting where there are no losers, only very important little individuals.

3. Kids need to feel cared for.

Something as simple as a daily routine can contribute to a child's sense of well-being. Clean clothes say "I care." Food in the refrigerator says it. Good meals say it—real meals spreading aromas through the house, not a constant diet of cardboard-wrapped meal deals gobbled down on the run. Help with homework or chores says it. Having a regular expected bedtime is important for learning the value of routine. Tuning into their stories at bedtime speaks it loud and clear. Allowing open schedules without structure can lead children to expect chaos and accept it as normal.

Like your kids, my children liked and disliked different foods. They enjoyed knowing that we cared about what did and didn't go into their lunches and what we cooked for dinner. Enough of the right foods speaks volumes about being cared for.

We've got to have a *high-touch* approach to our kids' lives rather than a *high-tech* one. Nowadays, technology can become addicting and distract our children and us from what's really important. It's true that it's a great tool, but we all need to have time-outs from our screens so we know what it's like to really connect. Our kids need many emotional touches during a day to be assured of our care: times when we listen, give guidance, draw boundaries, lend assistance, empathize with others, show support, and just participate in their world. While we can certainly check in with our teens by texting to show we care, we need to remember that these interactions are limiting. They don't allow for eye contact or facial expressions, and your face shows love better than an emoji.

A high-touch approach can take many forms. Use your creativity while looking for even more ways to make a difference in your children's lives. Every time you become involved in the daily routine and needs of your children, you send the message "I care about you." When you make continual sacrifices to meet your children's needs, you speak volumes of the same message. And your care feels so much better and meets deeper needs than the care of a paid sitter ever could.

Being available is one of the most important ways to make someone feel cared for. A friend still remembers the pain of not being available to her child at a critical time. She was working and couldn't be located when her son was badly injured at recess—he lost three teeth and suffered a fractured jaw. What did he need more than anything? The security of having his mother there to comfort him in his pain. What could substitute for her? Nothing.

And don't fool yourself, Mom. Nothing can substitute for you, either. When bad things happen to your children, you're the most important person in the world, and being available is the most important job you can have in the world.

How is it, then, that otherwise-intelligent parents feel they're showing their kids they love them when they constantly send messages to the contrary? They're too busy for their kids, too heavily scheduled, too stressed, or too tired to be interested. Or they have other things to do that are just too important to take time for the "little things." But little things add up.

How would you feel about someone who *said* you were important but didn't act like it? Or if someone tried to buy you off by giving you gifts to try to fill the gap? "I love you, but I don't have time for what's important to you" is a very confusing message. It hurts.

4. Kids need to develop good attitudes.

Our best efforts are needed to teach our children good attitudes. As your children grow up in your home, watching your example, what kinds of attitudes are they developing toward relationships, for instance? Are they viewing marriage as a positive commitment? Or are they becoming leery of entrusting themselves to a spouse? Are they learning to commit themselves to someone, to accept others unconditionally, to think the best?

When kids have good attitudes, good actions usually follow. If you have trouble with bad actions in your home, don't just discipline the actions; get to the root of the attitudes. And remember, attitudes are more caught than taught. What attitudes do you model when it comes to work, chores, caring for the family, sacrificing for others, authority, civil leaders, taxes, and your neighbors? Before you condemn your kids' attitudes, make sure you've examined the example you're modeling.

5. Kids need to develop good responses.

How we respond to the crises, threats, and inconveniences that come our way shows our kids the real us dealing with the real world. And every example we give them helps determine how they will respond to their own real world.

One time when our boys were little, we decided to earn extra money for something special. So we rose at dawn and drove to nearby berry fields to join the migrant workers harvesting the crop. After working about 30 minutes, we were approached by the foreman, who yelled at me as he wagged a long finger, "Get out of here, lady! We don't ever want to see you and these kids again!"

I was crushed, embarrassed, and insulted. I had no idea what we'd done wrong. We needed the money we would have earned, but I gathered the boys, set down our berries, and quietly started for the car. A moment later, the foreman came running up to us. He had mistaken us for another family that had caused trouble, he said. Now he apologized profusely and begged us to return. Because of our calm, respectful response, it became obvious we weren't the guilty party he had mistaken us for. Our kids took it all in.

Injustice comes in many ways. Kent once made a shot to win his district singles tennis championship in a high-school tournament, and the umpire made the call in his favor. But the opponent and his coach harassed the official and intimidated him until the call was reversed. The fans were shocked. The opponent prevailed. Kent lost this significant match. As we've told the boys so many times, life is not fair.

Kent's response was measured and noble. He was able to react well in the midst of the injustice and disappointment because his security didn't rest in that trophy. He had a healthy self-image, and his response to such an event had been formed in his nature long before the crisis. What showed on the outside was a reflection of what dwelt on the inside.

6. Kids need to develop good patterns.

Kids watch, listen, and question all we do in determining their own patterns and philosophies of life. They establish their work ethic from how we work. They learn priorities from how we spend our time and resources. They learn about God based on how we live out our faith. They watch how we handle everything, first to determine their own beliefs and later to question them to see if they're valid.

If you google "Children Learn What They Live," you'll find a famous poem written by Dorothy Law Nolte that captures beautifully just how big a difference we can make in our kids' lives. Here are two lines of this well-loved poem:

> *If a child lives with criticism,*
> *he learns to condemn. . . .*
> *If a child lives with security,*
> *he learns to have faith.*[5]

May we not rationalize the negatives of our behavior as we parent our kids. Remember, the Bible tells us "the heart is deceitful . . . and desperately sick" (Jeremiah 17:9).

Our culture is also deceitful: Don't let its subtle messages mesmerize you into thinking that mothering is a waste of your intelligent being. What messages are you hearing, and from whom? Take stock and remember your goal: developing children with solid self-esteem, character, and purpose.

Mom, you and I do make a difference. Moment by moment, as our children live and learn under our care, we influence the colors that add depth and richness to their lives. Our coloring greatly affects the final picture.

There's just one caveat: Although we need to do all we can to nurture our children, we cannot guarantee the outcome of their lives. As our kids become teens and young adults, they have the freedom to make their own choices. Some of those choices may be unhealthy, even if we have taught our kids good patterns and lived out our faith as best we can. Even God's children, Israel, repeatedly walked away from Him and disavowed His influence. Yet in spite of this possibility, we are called to show our children God's way to live, knowing that our influence *does* have a major impact.

Mom, right now, you have the power to be highly influential. Imagine the incredible difference you can make in your children's lives! Now isn't that exciting?

CHAPTER 5

OH, THEY'LL TURN OUT ALL RIGHT . . . WON'T THEY?

Sadly, no magic formulas can guarantee our children's future happiness. We can mother well and they may still make poor choices or meet unfortunate circumstances. But there are some basic, commonsense approaches that greatly improve the odds in favor of our kids' turning out well.

One time when Ryan was young, I planned a family dinner party for his birthday. We have a large extended family, so I've always been glad that our dining room table could accept five leaves. After cleaning the house and starting the meal, I stretched the table to its full length, set all the leaves in place, and hurried on with other preparations.

Before long, I heard a crash. There in the dining room lay

my beautiful, broken table. The extension rails had snapped under the weight of the leaves, and it had all collapsed in a heap on the floor. I had a birthday dinner to serve, and now I had no table to serve it on.

In my haste and distraction with other things, I had forgotten to add the fifth leg that was needed to support the center section whenever leaves were added. My intentions for the day had been excellent. I had a lot of other important things to attend to for the good of the whole family. But that was no excuse. If I hadn't been so distracted, my common sense would have told me extra support was needed—now. That's how the table was designed.

But I was in such a hurry that I just didn't think about the consequences. As I often say, if I'd just gotten "smart enough soon enough," I would have recognized the danger and taken steps to prevent it. And similarly, that's what we moms must do as well—foresee dangers for our kids and take action to prevent the trouble. It's not all that different from maintaining our cars or eating a good diet. It's called preventive maintenance, and it's critical.

Many years ago, an American Medical Association's report on increased violence, injury, and substance abuse among the nation's youth concluded with this statement: "Parents need to wake up and pay more attention to their children."[1]

That statement must be even truer today, since the opportunities for making bad choices have only increased with the addition of the Internet, social media, more potent drugs, and legalization of marijuana in some states. Think about access to pornography: It's never been easier. According to studies in the United States and abroad, about 40 percent of teens and preteens visit sexually explicit websites either deliberately or accidentally.[2]

Our society is plagued with increasing problems, some of which didn't exist or barely existed when I was growing up: road rage; mass shootings; porn and drug addictions; youth obesity and eating disorders; sexual perversion and promiscuity on display in easily obtainable books and films, and on the Internet; sexual identification issues and sex changes.

Who could have ever conceived of something called "swatting"? Now it's in the news; after a dispute during online gaming, a 25-year-old man lied to authorities so a SWAT team would be sent to the home of another gamer. The 25-year-old sent police to the wrong address, and an innocent man was killed.[3]

With these new kinds of dangers and issues, our kids are overwhelmed, and we're overwhelmed. Natural coping mechanisms or instincts seem insufficient for everything children face today. What in the world are we to do?

The answer is almost too easy to believe. It's so obvious, it's overlooked. The answer is in our children's *hearts* and *spirits*, and the home is where the remedies are worked in and the results are first lived out.

And make no mistake: Mothers have lifelong influence on their children's hearts and minds. Science has even shown that a mom's love improves her child's brain and the ability to regulate emotions.

A 2016 study revealed that a mother's love increased the size of an important part of the brain: the hippocampus, which affects the functioning of learning, memory, and emotion regulation. Scientists studied 127 children and their interactions with their mothers, taking brain scans of the children through school age and early adolescence. The study found that the more maternal support a child received during the preschool years, the larger the child's hippocampus grew. And apparently, a bigger hippocampus is a better one![4]

The study showed that a larger hippocampus is associated with healthier regulation of emotions in adolescence and concluded that "early childhood maternal support fosters healthy childhood brain development and emotion functioning."[5]

"This study suggests there's a sensitive period when the brain responds more to maternal support," said Joan Luby, the first author of the study and a Washington University child psychiatrist at St. Louis Children's Hospital.[6]

Moms, we can *hope* our kids turn out all right and don't become statistics . . . or we can *do* something about it, something to prevent trouble.

Our kids need our acceptance and attention, enough attention that we pick up on what hurts, intimidates, and tempts them. We can't get that just by sharing rooms in a house; we can't communicate unconditional love by leaving notes on the refrigerator. We have to share time, experiences, and our hearts.

If our kids get the acceptance from us that they so desperately need, they won't likely go looking for it elsewhere. And kids do need acceptance. They need identity—self-identity, not just (in our case) "being one of the Weber boys." They're looking for affirmation of what they say, how they dress, their opinions, and their mannerisms.

Kids must have affirmation or they won't grow to healthy adulthood. Children probably fear two things more than anything else—isolation and rejection. If we leave them alone, they'll go seeking the company of someone else. If we reject them, they'll look for a place to be accepted. And it won't matter how bad the place is. It won't matter how poor the morals. Any place can feel like a haven if isolation and rejection are dispelled.

Kids need their own space, but they don't want to feel lonely or isolated. We have to watch out for the difference. We have to be careful not to barge into their space, but we also have to make sure they know we're there and available if they need us. If loneliness does start to set in, knowing we're there for them may be all the comfort they need.

And then there's rejection. We all remember rejection, don't we? When someone pointed out our mistakes, commented on our hair or clothing, laughed at something we did?

We all hate to be embarrassed. So why is it we so frequently embarrass our kids and then chide them for being too sensitive when they groan, "Mom!"

We can make our kids feel rejected in so many ways. After all, they're still trying to determine who they are and what they believe. Any remarks and attitudes toward their words or actions can be interpreted as a rejection of *them*, not what they're doing. We need to be sensitive to that and make sure our impact on them is positive, not negative.

Rejection can be sensed in our tone of voice, our body language, that certain look. Kids may feel rejected when we can't afford time to be with them or the money to provide something they think is important (especially if they see money going in a lot of other directions for *our* pleasure).

For me, it was difficult having no money for even basics as my kids grew up. We didn't have many hand-me-downs or money for things most kids had. After watching *Chariots of Fire* as a seventh grader, Kent decided that someday, somehow he would study at Oxford or Cambridge in England. Long story short, he attended Oxford and Durham Universities in England (on his tennis pro money and an International Rotary Scholarship), and all the boys graduated from Wheaton College in Illinois debt-free. Isn't it interesting how all of this happened even though we had no money? It was a God thing for sure.

When we visited Kent in England using frequent-flier tickets, I felt bad when we arrived and saw our six-foot-five-inch-tall son looking like a skeleton. I told him, "We are going out right now and getting you something to eat." He hadn't had money for a lot of food, but he wasn't bitter, just totally happy. When I apologized to him for our lack of provision throughout the years, his response was "Mom, I had everything I needed."

In addition to affirmation, children need guidance. Why do kids have sex at such early ages? Their curiosity outweighs their instruction, so let's instruct them and provide scenarios of consequences. They need to understand a standard—what standard are you teaching them?

Why do kids fall into substance abuse? One reason is that they don't know all of the dangers or what might happen as they become involved. So let's educate them. They don't have the self-confidence to say no, so let's build up their sense of identity and give them firm permission to push back against peer pressure. They need acceptance, or they just might do some of the dumbest things to get it. So let's shower them with acceptance and a feeling that they can trust us and the protective boundaries we provide.

Guidance includes informing our kids about the danger and possibilities of sexual abuse so they develop an awareness of predators. Let's be keenly aware of any remote possibilities for sexual abuse and guard against it.

One of my guys had a coach I was leery of. He wanted to coach my son, one-on-one, so the two would be alone. I didn't feel comfortable about it and gave my son a strong warning speech. My son stayed on the offensive, and nothing bad happened. But six months later, that coach was found guilty for sexually abusing multiple kids and was stripped of his job and reputation.

Because sexual abuse is way too common, Mom, you need to know how to protect your children. Watch out for predators and teach your kids to be leery and to run. I suggest you do some reading to understand the minds of sexual offenders. It's shocking to see how large numbers of school-age children are experiencing sexual abuse at the hands of highly respected people.

These offenders work at gaining the trust of children, grooming them by winning their minds before going after their bodies. They isolate their victims with secrecy and push boundaries. Offenders might offer gifts and flattery and will continue to push their way into your children's lives. (I've had good families share with me how this issue has surprisingly crept into their lives.)

If your child should become a victim of sexual abuse, do get help from knowledgeable sources (carefully selected counselors and books) and realize that your child can overcome with the power of God. The Focus on the Family counseling line (1-855-771-4357) can offer you a referral to Christian counselors in your area and provide a onetime consultation at no cost.

Do all you can to prevent trouble and bad situations for your kids. Don't wait till you've been robbed to install an alarm system. We can't take the "wait and see" approach. We have to take preventive measures all along the way. Are you setting specific guidelines for the character qualities your teens need to look for when choosing a date and talking with them about why these are important? Why wait until we see our kids out with the wrong crowd? Why wait until we sense things aren't healthy with a boyfriend or girlfriend? Why wait until they become secretive or avoid us? And if someone close happens to warn you of some deviant or destructive behavior in one of your kids, don't pridefully ignore it and refuse to take steps to eradicate it. The consequences could be dire.

Instead, let's anticipate some of the problems and show we're on our kids' sides. Let's communicate, discussing the difficult issues kids face while they're still theory. Let's make sure we're both available and approachable. Let's not wait till we see red flags before we begin to develop a plan. Preventing negative experiences requires positive planning and work.

I clearly remember a time when Stu and I had to take preventive steps with one of our sons. When he was 13, there was a kid on his soccer team that he was enthralled with. The phone rang regularly as the two buddies stayed in constant touch. Whenever there was an event to attend, they wanted to do it together. It's great to have friends, but from my perspective, this kid was not a good influence. He had a bad attitude, he didn't respond well to authority, and his parents were never home, where there were unacceptable magazines handy. The more I learned, the easier it was to put a stop to that friendship, and quickly. The bad habits were spilling over to our son's life. Our son wasn't receptive to our decision, but years later he has thanked us repeatedly for taking him away from that bad influence.

In addition to providing acceptance, attention, and guidance, we need to validate our kids' feelings and help them learn how to regulate their emotions if we want them to turn out all right.

For example, anger is a common issue in a child's life. When parents see this emotion blossoming, the wise mom and dad will help their child develop the skill of dealing with anger. As you do this with your children, you'll be helping them handle the many frustrations that will surface in years to come.

So how do you help them regulate their anger? First, you must validate their feelings. Make sure you create a comfort zone for conversation so they feel safe to share with you how they feel. That means you don't immediately try to fix the situation, offer them lighthearted responses, or ignore their feelings.

Mom, instead of telling your children that they shouldn't feel angry, tell them "I hear you." You want to communicate that you care. Let them know that you're going to help them work on this. This process can also defuse that anger because they'll feel they have an ally.

If they come to you with anger about something, make sure your response doesn't catastrophize the situation. That won't help your children, either. If your response is wild, you may be teaching them to dwell on an injustice done toward them, fostering the idea that they'll never survive this bad situation and teaching them to be insecure.

As you help them regulate their anger, you are helping them know that holding on to anger isn't good for them, and that you can't allow them to go on hurting. Just keep validating your children's emotions and teaching them to develop good self-control. Remember, Ephesians 4:26 says, "Be angry and do not sin." If a child doesn't learn how to deal with anger in a healthy way, it can result in undesirable behavior.

Mom, your impact is enormous. Your mind-set as you raise your children is powerful, and you can use that power to steer your children's lives in positive directions. Live the motto of the children's book *The Little Engine That Could* by Watty Piper. As you claim, "I think I can, I think I can," you will model empowerment for your children.

Let's be sure we're providing the right atmosphere in our homes, making them places that encourage good things and help bad things dissolve before they can get a foothold. Let's be careful to watch what's going on. Let's be backers instead of critics, and we'll see the daily crises lose momentum and fall away.

To dispel the negative things in life, we need to add a lot to the positive side. Let's have fun with our kids. Let's show them that we enjoy them. Let's make our times together happy times. Let's live our moments with them to the fullest.

Remember, Mom, have that accepting tone, and make your home a happy place to be, not just a stopover between events. When your kids face the dark moments of growing up, they'll run to the one place where they feel secure and accepted. Let's make sure that's your home.

CHAPTER 6

WHAT IS NURTURING, ANYWAY?

WHILE DINING OUT with my husband, I overheard a nicely dressed woman pouring her heart out to her friend about the pain and rejection she still felt because of her childhood, even though she must have been at least 65 years old. When she was young, this woman's mother was never home. The girl was pretty much left on her own and given responsibilities a mother usually assumed.

Even decades later, she was talking about her resentment and depression over this lack of nurturing and the poor self-image it had generated. Her strong feelings of abandonment haunted her fiercely. Oh, the lasting effect that lingers when a child is not nurtured!

Robert Lewis and William Hendricks write of an even-more-tragic example of having not been nurtured. A young man seemingly had all the advantages in the world. He came from a famous and well-to-do family. He had graduated at the top of his class from one of the most highly regarded universities. He was a successful businessman with a wife and family. And yet all that was overshadowed by his great unmet needs from childhood.

In 1949, actress Mercedes McCambridge won an Academy Award. I'm sure she felt on top of the world. Certainly she was at the top of her career. The whole industry applauded what she had accomplished on film.

But her son, John, didn't join the party. To the outside world, the McCambridge home glittered. But for a son who needed a mother, this family was anything but a success. Even though John later became a very successful financial broker, his life was haunted by the deficits his upbringing had left within him. In the spring of 1989, he exploded. Before murdering his own wife and two children and then committing suicide, he penned these words to his famous mother:[1]

"I was essentially raised by live-in maids and relatives. You never were there for me. I tried to get your love through academic achievement, gifts, and, finally, enormous personal risk. You love to tell the story of the boy who got paid to babysit himself. That means I was left alone. Alone! At five years old, in his little suit and hat, flying across the country alone. Alone! Is this clear to you, mom? . . . There is nothing more to say."[2]

Obviously, these illustrations show what nurturing is *not*. Let's look at the dictionary definition of *nurturing* and its synonyms—*nourishing, sustaining, supporting, feeding, fostering, cherishing, educating, training*, and *rearing*. Doing all of these things for my children sounds like a pretty good calling to me. And it's not only a good calling; it's also a way to prevent the physical, mental, and spiritual pain that's created without nurture. Research shows what can happen without nurture.

In fact, scientific studies now tell us that nurture plays a critical role in brain development.

More than a decade of research on children raised in institutions shows that "neglect is awful for the brain," says Charles Nelson, a professor of pediatrics at Harvard Medical School and Boston Children's Hospital. Without someone who is a reliable source of attention, affection and stimulation, he says, "the wiring of the brain goes awry." The result can be long-term mental and emotional problems.[3]

Even a child's physical health as an adult is affected by adverse experiences in childhood. According to The Adverse Childhood Experiences Study, "An increasing body of evidence documents the robust relationship between adverse experiences in early childhood and a host of complications, both medical and psychological, that manifest throughout childhood and later in life."[4]

When I was growing up, we frequently went to a certain office to pay our bills. I'll always remember the sign on the wall that said, "Think ahead." The last four letters of *ahead* were written off to the side, showing how the designer of the sign didn't "think ahead"! Nurturing thinks ahead for our kids.

Listen to what Dr. Gail Gross, a human behavior expert and child development specialist, said about how nurturing affects a person's future:

> Although your genes lay out a blueprint for your
> potential development, they do not determine
> the way in which you will grow. Instead, it is the
> environment your parents create that instructs and
> directs your genes by enhancing some and turning
> off others. In other words, parents are the true gene
> therapists. . . .
>
> Moreover, contrary to what you've been told (or
> sold), your child doesn't necessarily need special
> teachers, lessons, or flashcards. But what he does
> need is a supporting, stimulating environment . . .

and, above all, specific bonding experiences with you, his parent.

Why are these important? Because an environment that is deliberately filled with warmth and stimulation fosters the neural connections in his brain responsible for thought, emotion, and behavior.

Meeting your child's needs, soothing him with your voice and your touch, reading a book, cuddling, or any activity that involves nurturing, will do much to enhance your baby's emotional well-being, temperament, personality, and ability to cope with stress, and whether he reaches his overall potential.[5]

Yes, our children need their black-and-white lines colored in as we've discussed. On a basic level, it's fairly elementary to ensure the physical development. But there are other spaces to fill that are out of sight and more difficult to nurture. We need to color in these interior spaces to give a child's life dimension. As mothers, we are artists, whether we realize it or not. We shape the future of these little children as we color in the spaces.

Being an effective "colorer" takes all the intelligence and understanding we can gather. It also demands a good attitude and a proper perspective as we remember "children are a heritage from the LORD; the fruit of the womb a reward" (Psalm 127:3). It would be helpful if the Bible included one lengthy book presenting easy step-by-step instructions in nurturing. However, it seems that God deemed it a fruitful experience for us to gather principles from throughout Scripture to acquire the understanding we need. Proverbs 28:5 says, "Those who seek the LORD understand all things" (NASB).

When our children need help with homework questions about geometry theorems and chemical equations, those subjects may be beyond our immediate grasp. We'll probably have to dig through the textbook or watch a YouTube tutorial before we can help with the problem.

In a like manner, God will grant wisdom to those of us who dig in the Scriptures and pursue a relationship with Him. God wants to give us understanding so we can nurture well, so we can discern the intents of our children's hearts, so we can make fair parenting decisions and set firm boundaries. With the stakes so high, we must fill our mental reservoirs with skillful tips and principles of wisdom from God. We can't know too much to nurture a child well.

Just as we would pursue the best medical help when needed, we'll also want to go to the best sources of information about molding our children's lives. So search the Scriptures. Read good books—adopt the good and let the other go. As you apply creativity, energy, and skill to the work of nurturing your children, your family can't help but win. You'll want to channel the talents you might possess and the learning you have acquired into enhancing your child's thinking, attitudes, and actions.

Obviously, there are some differences of opinion about

what nurturing means in our society. Many parents believe that babysitters and material things are all a child really needs. I heard one movie star announce that all she needed to raise a child was a room, a few toys, and a babysitter. We know that there's much more to it than that!

What those people don't know is this founding principle of raising a child: "Whatever one sows, that will he also reap" (Galatians 6:7). Although there can be natural disasters along the way, the law of the harvest remains. What we put into our children affects how they grow and mature. We parents need to focus on the principle of personal responsibility of sowing and all that the nurturing process entails.

Some moms may think nurturing really isn't too important right now. After all, the baby is so young, it won't matter if Mom's busy doing "more important" or "more fulfilling" things. Others whose kids are a little older may think their kids look pretty well grounded, that they're past the nurturing stage. You might be surprised—we need to learn from those who know better.

Let's learn from Dr. Charles Raison, who was CNN Health's mental health expert and an associate professor of psychiatry when he wrote this in 2012:

> Over the last decade a string of scientific discoveries has shown that the biology driving mental illness has at least as much to do with the environment as with chemicals or genetic inheritance. And it increasingly appears that the single most powerful environmental

factor is the love—or its lack—that children receive from their parents. . . . I say this based on a thousand studies. . . . We underestimate our power as parents at our children's peril. . . . One generation full of deeply loving parents would change the brain of the next generation, and with that, the world.[6]

Since you're reading this book, my guess is that you want to nurture your child well. Good for you! In the next chapter, we'll take a detailed look at ways to do that.

CHAPTER 7

THE NURTURING PROCESS, PART 1

As I GREW UP amid apple orchards in Yakima, Washington, I saw good examples of what nurturing is all about. I watched year-round as farmers faithfully tended their trees. They never quit. They were always doing something to nurture and maintain their crops. They knew that the ongoing process is important if there's to be a good crop in the fall.

You don't plant an orchard and then say, "Mission accomplished. Time to relax." And you don't raise confident kids that way, either.

Being orchard growers would be hard for some of us, because it's difficult to wait for results. But that's the way apple growing works. There are few immediate results and rewards. It takes patience and diligence. And it takes confidence that the harvest is coming. That's the way nurturing works too. Nurturing is a combination of time and attention. If the formula doesn't have both ingredients, or if they're not properly balanced, nurturing doesn't happen.

As a child, I noticed that when a new section of orchard was planted, the young trees were carefully dug in and staked. A ground cover was planted between the rows to be tilled in later to provide nutrients for the roots. And in our dry climate, irrigation was used extensively. The trees were set in good soil and provided with the support and nutrition needed to ensure their growth.

The same approach applies to our kids. It's critical that we place them in an environment where they're provided with the right support and protection and given an environment where they can begin to grow without feeling trampled, overshadowed, or overlooked.

A tree grower doesn't just hope there's enough nourishment available for his trees to flourish. By his efforts, he *ensures* it. Our kids need to have their innermost beings nourished and refreshed as much as they need their bodies fed to ensure growth. Can we take any more casual approach to meeting their needs than the farmer does to meeting the needs of his trees?

The promise of a healthy product and thus income for the next year motivated the growers' work. They didn't complain that it took too long or that each phase was unimportant. They didn't take long breaks or neglect any measures, no matter how small. Farmers remained acutely aware of the consequences they would experience if they didn't nurture their trees and follow the right process.

Not only that, they knew healthy trees would bear fruit for decades. In the same way, your efforts as a committed and nurturing mother will outlive you and affect future generations of your family. Consider the apple tree that's still growing at the birthplace of Isaac Newton, the scientist who discovered gravity after watching an apple fall from his tree. That tree in England is still being pruned and still producing fruit four hundred years after it was planted.[1] Granted, it's an unusual case, but the tree was tended to for generations by the Woolerton family, tenant farmers who lived in the house from 1733 to 1947. Their care and provision for the tree kept it alive and flourishing.[2]

Provision means supplying or furnishing. Its etymological roots lie significantly in the Latin word *pro-video*, meaning to "look ahead." Like the farmer, the nurturing mom needs to look ahead and continue the process of nurturing if she is to expect good results, a good harvest. Moms, you look ahead when you can anticipate and fulfill your children's short-term and long-term needs.

As you study the illustration titled "Process Required for a Good Harvest," you'll see how important your involvement as a nurturing mother is to the harvest of good character in your child.

The farmer must provide the right care, support, and protection of the tree, and all with the right timing. In the same way, you must also provide the proper care, support, and protection of your child, and with the right timing.

If you look at the tree illustration, you'll see that the process of caring for a tree requires attention to myriad details. If any link in the process is omitted, the tree's foundational roots suffer devastating effects. The consequences then affect

Process Required for a Good Harvest

The Farmer
must provide the right

Care: soil prep, planting, cultivating, watering

Support: staking, fertilizing, inspecting

Protection: weeding, pruning, spraying, smudging

Timing: thinning, propping, picking (not according to the almanac)

to meet the crop's needs at just the RIPE moment

If the farmer is not there . . . there is not much hope for a great harvest.

The Nurturing Mom
must provide the right

Care: dimensionally (physically, mentally, emotionally, and spiritually)

Support: solid foundation, a discerning parent, connection, a training plan

Protection: boundaries/hedges, supervision, advice, prevention procedures, discipline

Timing: "scheduled availability" during windows of opportunity

to meet the child's needs at just the RIPE moment

If Mom is not there . . . serious deficiencies affect the harvest of character and self-respect.

Are we promoting a quality harvest?

(barring flood, freeze, or conditions beyond our control)

the farmer's harvest. Ignoring or improperly handling the process will cause painful loss. I use this example to show that a mother's nurturing also needs to be ongoing, careful, and done with much thought and insight for the long term.

The illustration first notes the care process. We'll take a close look at that in chapter 8. In this chapter, let's consider the support, protection, and timing elements of the nurturing process.

Support

The farmer supports his crop by cultivating his roots with care: He stakes them, fertilizes them, inspects them. As our farmer friend John says of his tree crop, "The value is in the roots. When the roots are healthy, the tree can fight off disease and be strong."

A mom first supports her child by developing a *solid foundation*, the root system that keeps a child steady and strong as he or she grows and faces the complicated circumstances of life. As you read in earlier chapters, mothers are the critical link to developing a deep root system: Those roots provide a child with emotional security, a healthy self-concept, a growing brain, and even the ability to love and trust others throughout his or her life.

A strong root system holds up a tree, and the roots we provide for our children must also be strong. Because this root system is so important, many approaches to counseling rely heavily on learning about it—the family of origin. How the father and mother lived, and how they related to one another and their children, give tremendous insights into why children approach and live their lives the way they do. It's so much easier for a tree with a weak root system to topple over in a storm. Mom, when you're nurturing your child, you are developing a healthy root system.

Another important way to support your child is to practice *discernment*. Hebrews 5:13-14 (NASB) helps us see that people who develop spiritual maturity are those "who because of practice have their senses trained to discern good and evil." Just as we can physically work out in a gym, we can also "work out our minds" in the Word of righteousness, strengthening our skills as discerning nurturers.

Proverbs 31:26 describes this type of nurturer: "She opens her mouth with wisdom, and the teaching of kindness is on her tongue." In a very broad description, that same chapter in Proverbs goes on to refer to this nurturer's support work: "She looks well to the ways of her household and does not eat the bread of idleness" (31:27). Mom, thousands of your actions translate into messages of emotional support.

A nurturing mom will discern how each child is gifted and how she might best channel these gifts. Writing about the influence of her mother, Ingrid Trobisch quotes her mother as saying, "'Look! That child is like a budding flower; every day a new petal unfolds.' From her sensitivity I learned to recognize one child's artistic nature, another's love for music, another's gift for hospitality. She helped me ask the right questions to bring out their different personalities."[3]

The way my friend Rebecca describes mothering points to her discernment about the uniqueness of each of her children.

I enjoy flowers very much. When my children were little, I likened them to flowers. Geraniums, for instance, can endure hot temperatures and direct sunlight. In fact, that's what it takes for them to produce their brilliant blossoms. Others, like impatiens, require constant shade. Direct sunlight is detrimental. Their blooms can be just as vibrant as the geraniums when they're allowed to grow where they're intended to grow.

The same is true for our children. I'm convinced the best things we can do for our children in their early years is to be in constant study and observation of them—not to constantly scrutinize their behavior, but to learn, both for our own sake and for theirs. . . .

How Jason reacts to a situation is totally different from Tim's reaction. Some things matter a lot more to Emily than they do to either of the boys. The kids are the healthiest, and we have the best relationships with them, when we understand what's important to each one and what intimidates each one.

Gary and I thoroughly enjoy our children. Is it because they are exceptional? I don't think so. I think it's because we've tried to be good students of our children.

The discerning mom can further her abilities to nurture her child by taking advantage of parent support groups. When I was privileged to be an advisor to one such group, I watched women gain understanding and encourage each other to persevere in rearing their children. I recommend you find a group, read books on personality traits and talents, or maybe even take a parenting class or two. Everybody wins through your developed discernment.

Providing adequate support also requires connecting with your child. As with electricity, when there is *connection*, there is power. Consider these words regarding the life-changing influence of connection from *High Risk: Children Without a Conscience* by Ken Magid and Carole A. McKelvey:

> If the first relationship a baby has does not set the stage for trust, then later relationships cannot be based on trust. The baby learns from the first relationship what he can and cannot expect from others. If there is no healthy give and take, the baby will not know how to give and take with others. Unattached children do not grow socially. They have great difficulty learning to build any kind of relationship.[4]

Moms, your ultimate example of connection is the Lord God. Isaiah 66:13 says, "As one whom his mother comforts, so I will comfort you." The Holy Spirit is to us what we are to our children. John 14:16-18, 26, and 27 tells us that He will

- be with us,
- not leave us as orphans,
- come to us,
- teach us all things,
- bring to our remembrance all He said, and
- leave peace with us.

What an opportunity we have to connect to the strong support levels God has for us. And isn't it interesting that God Himself used the original word *paraclete*, "one who is called beside," to describe how the Holy Spirit functions as the nurturing mother functions?

Nurturing is serious business that produces long-term effects for society, so supporting your child's growth requires a training plan. While creating and implementing a plan is challenging, to say the least, it will help ensure the quality formation of good attitudes, responses, and patterns for living.

Romans 10:14 reminds us that to learn, we must be taught. Interestingly enough, we see that river otters can't swim until their mothers teach them. Children are little copycats, ongoing copy machines, producing duplicates of everything they observe. Scary, wouldn't you say? What model are we providing for them? What character-developing plan do we have for them?

Great results don't just happen, and they don't develop with crash courses, either. So be intentional about nurturing over the long haul. For example, you could consider placing a strong focus on one character quality each year, to make sure you're not hitting and missing with your efforts.

As you provide this type of support, you may begin to see the fruit of good character in your children. But that doesn't mean your supporting role is over. The process is a continual one.

As apple trees begin to bear fruit, their young branches are often too fragile to bear all the weight and must be propped up and supported. The same is true of our children. When their loads get too heavy for them to bear alone, we need to prop them up and support them. To do that, we have to be there and be aware. Encouraging healthy growth isn't just a matter of proper launching, but also of staying alongside, walking with, keeping close. You don't want that branch to break before you get to it; otherwise there is damage and no apple crop.

Protection

Keeping that branch from breaking requires *protection*. Just as farmers stay aware so they can protect the fragile tree branches, you will also need to stay aware so you can protect your child from various adverse environmental influences.

I remember how one of our sons had an especially hard time in middle school. One of his teachers didn't seem to like him much. That constantly discouraged him. His athletic efforts weren't very successful that year, either, which further darkened his outlook. He was always down on himself and resolved to quit more than once.

His little branches of self-confidence were too fragile to bear the weight of this period alone, so I vowed to give an extra measure of myself to him. Even though he refuted my compliments and ignored my praise in that season, I worked hard to be positive and keep finding right things he was doing that I could applaud. I told him how wonderful and special he was, and that I knew he could make it.

It took a couple of years to get him out of that slump. The extra effort was exhausting and frustrating. Yet I'm convinced that if I hadn't determined to prop him up at that point, his life could easily have taken a lasting negative turn.

Protecting your children also means making *boundaries and hedges*. Proverbs 22:6 says, "Train up a child in the way he should go; even when he is old he will not depart from it." The Hebrew meaning of *train* is significant—it's translated in English as the *continual active initiation of life boundaries*.

This verse implies that parents must employ a great deal of effort to train up a child.

Continual obviously means that your training is constantly happening and not something you can check off your list. *Active* means you will need to make conscious and deliberate choices in a brisk manner as you lay boundary lines for your children.

Boundaries are lines that are not to be crossed. Children need to know that as they choose to cross the boundary line, there are consequences to expect on the other side. Mom, be diligent in making sure the consequences happen so your children learn you mean business. Enforcing boundaries, as difficult as that can be at times, can keep children from feeling entitled to their own way, a way that can harm them in the end.

There are the simple and obvious boundaries you teach your children, such as not going into the street so they don't get hit by a car. But the boundaries become more complicated as your children grow. You'll be initiating boundaries concerning their friends and what they are exposed to in a movie or on the Internet. You'll need to set boundaries regarding where they are allowed to go and how late they are allowed to stay out, how they are allowed to talk to you and the kind of respect that is expected.

Maybe you'll need to set boundaries to address the kind of clothing they wear because their choices could send wrong messages, or how much time they can spend on their phones or computers, and which filters and programs must be used to keep them from unsafe websites or from harmful apps. You can and must establish boundaries for your children.

Just like a guardrail that kept my husband and me from going over a cliff in an icy, windy snowstorm in Austria years ago, the guardrails you set up in your children's lives every day can keep them from unpleasant and horrible disasters that could wreck their lives. Your ongoing nurturing and attention to detail in their lives, your *continual active initiation of life boundaries*, provides the support your children need to thrive.

These days, boundaries are vital when it comes to technology. There are just too many dangers online for your children. Consider these statistics:

- Teens who spend more than three hours per school day on social networks are 110 percent more likely to be cyberbullied.[5]

- More than 60 percent of teens say cyberbullying affects their ability to learn and feel safe at school.[6]

- Fifty percent of teens surveyed by Common Sense Media in 2016 said they were addicted to their mobile devices.[7]

- People who use social media excessively may be more prone to anxiety, depressive symptoms, and stress.[8]

The average age a child is given a smartphone is 10; just think of the boundaries required by that parental decision. Daniel Huerta, Focus on the Family's vice president of parenting and youth, has this to say about smartphones and children: "I have found that many parents, whose children already have computer privileges, feel a cultural pressure to get their kids a cellphone. But a 10-year-old brain is not ready for the digital decisions that today's smartphones introduce."[9]

Moms, this is why boundaries are needed. But studies show that only 39 percent of parents use online filtering and monitoring software, and only 16 percent of parents use the parental-restriction functions on their kids' personal devices.[10]

This is an area where parents need to increase communication with their children, so their phones, video games, or some other social media option doesn't dominate their kids' minds. A nurturing mother will monitor her children's access to technology carefully, and not simply let them see and participate in an unguarded environment.

You can also protect your child by establishing *prevention* measures. Why wait until there are serious issues to deal with when you can set up a wise way now? You'll need some weed killer for any weeds that will pop up. Start by preventing the weeds of negative cultural trends from surrounding and overtaking your child. Some of these trends include no work ethic, no consequences, no absolute right or wrong, no responsibility, no discipline, no shame or condemnation, no accounting for differences (sameness demanded), no appreciation for the rule of law, no commitment in marriage, no morals, no respect, no innate gender appreciation, no losing allowed (everybody gets a trophy). We have a lot to think about as we work to protect our kids from nonbiblical influences.

A nurturing mom provides the right support and protection. Doesn't it feel right that we were made to be the nurturers? Our husbands are wired differently. They're made to conquer, to accomplish, to overcome. Their challenges often bring more measurable responses and immediate results. Our children will grow best as we each live out what we were best designed for.

Moms, we're the ones who create the climate, the security, the safety zone. We're the ones who provide the steady support and encouragement—it's part of our protection process for them.

Timing

We can fool ourselves at times, thinking that being available for our kids according to our preferred schedules is going to meet our kids' needs. But we're simply unable to predict when a window of opportunity to discuss some important subject is going to present itself. We cannot know when a child will decide to share some deep hurt that requires our response. You just can't plan some things—children have to be ready to talk or listen, and we don't know when that moment will happen. We just have to be available on their timetables. This is a hard assignment for us.

An absentee orchard grower wouldn't be very effective. He couldn't just schedule routine maintenance without being there to inspect the trees and evaluate their needs. He couldn't simply leave orders to set out heaters on some certain date so the fruit wouldn't freeze if he weren't aware of the temperature in his orchard from day to day, hour to hour. And he couldn't choose the day to begin harvesting based on an almanac. Without being there and being aware, he'd never have much hope of reaping a good harvest. He must protect those crops.

Why, then, are absentee parents convinced they can automatically "schedule maintenance" for their kids to ensure all their needs are met? The right kind of toy, the right sports club to attend, or the right extracurricular activities won't ensure well-balanced, healthy kids or take the place of being there for their children at the right time.

If kids are always in a group setting, where does individual pruning take place? Individual encouragement? Individual correction? And if there's no time for nurturing, how do we expect our kids to become all they can be?

Being a nurturing mother is a lot of work, and the job requires an enormous amount of wisdom and discernment. Providing the right support, protection, and timing so you can sow the seeds of a good harvest is a high calling, one that's critical for your children.

In the next chapter, we'll take an in-depth look at the remaining element of the process required for a good harvest: care.

CHAPTER 8

THE NURTURING PROCESS, PART 2

MICHELLE BEAULAURIER of Burlingame, California, one of nine children, wrote the following to her mother, who was questioning her own "at-home" value: "I would not be where I am today had you not been where you were! You were my support system, my encourager, my peace, and my challenger to go for it and to use my talents. You were always there to point out my special, God-given talents, so that I could reflect upon them and put them into use."[1]

Michelle's comments show that her mother provided multifaceted care for her. This mom undoubtedly went "below the surface" of her daughter's most apparent needs, meeting her psychological and spiritual needs as well. Unfortunately,

Am I nurturing my child beyond the obvious physical realm?

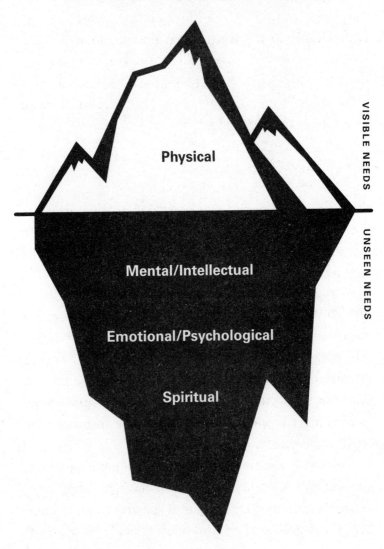

many incredibly intelligent moms act only on what they see with their eyes and focus only on the externals of life.

A nurturing mom, however, provides the right kind of thorough care that goes deeper. I'm not saying this is easy. Far from it! Daily life requires us to pay close attention to myriad issues. Every day we must decide where our strongest focus should be. We could use more eyes, ears, and intuitiveness— as well as more hours in a day—to address the many details demanding our attention.

Four Facets of Nurturing Care

The right type of care is multifaceted and involves four realms: the *physical realm*, the *mental/intellectual realm*, the *emotional/ psychological realm*, and the *spiritual realm*. We need to care for our children in all of these dimensions, but we must realize that in three of the four realms the needs are unseen.

The Physical Realm of Nurturing

Nurturing in the physical realm is somewhat easy because the needs are visible. Shelter, food to eat, and clothes to wear are obvious necessities. Being physically around to drive our children to their activities and attending to their health care are just a few of the needs that present themselves in a straightforward manner.

Yet even in the physical sphere, we can go the extra mile with our care. It takes work to prepare the right kinds of food and present them nicely. My friend Christy takes that simple need for meals and uses it to make her family feel especially loved. On her blog, *Back to the Table with Grace*, she teaches women to honor their families with special presentations that require extra loving effort. Of course, preparing these types of touches won't be possible all the time.

Have you noticed that in Scripture, so much of what is really important takes place around the table? Let's not underestimate the value that comes from preparing and sharing food together. At our house, we have a large table that can serve 14 to 18 people. We've served many dinners and enjoyed meals together with others, which teaches children to go and do likewise in their adult lives.

Generally speaking, caring for your child in the physical realm should be done in balance. Too little physical care reflects abuse or selfishness when we consistently ignore the needs of our families in favor of our own. Overindulgence, on the other hand, is just as destructive and leads to us spoiling our kids. Giving our children too many things decreases their appreciation for the benefits of work and reduces their incentive to provide a few things for themselves. Pushing a child to reach for physical perfection by demanding the best in appearance or the top spot at beauty pageants and athletic competitions counteracts healthy nurturing, no matter how well-intentioned the parent may be.

The Mental/Intellectual Realm of Nurturing

When we delve beneath the surface of our children's physical needs, we find the mental realm of nurturing. How do we nurture our kids' minds?

Studies indicate that parents can affect their children's IQ, interests, and abilities simply by reading aloud to them. According to early education expert and author Betty Bardige, "Reading aloud to young children is not only one of the best activities to stimulate language and cognitive skills; it also builds motivation, curiosity, and memory."[2]

Research shows that when you read aloud to your children, you are exposing them to more words, which improves vocabulary, grammar, sentence structure, and general knowledge. Vocabulary is closely related to academic success, and it's a key area on IQ tests. In fact, one study shows that as early as age two, children who are read to regularly display greater language comprehension, larger vocabularies, and higher cognitive skills than their peers.[3]

The year my husband was deployed in a combat zone, I enjoyed practicing this concept with our eight-month-old son, Kent, after I read the book *Give Your Child a Superior Mind*. I'll never know what specific good my efforts did, but Kent is a smart guy who's earned degrees from Wheaton, Durham, and Oxford. (Let me add that there are smart, successful people in the world who do not have degrees; I don't have one, for example, but have managed to author books and become successful in real estate.)

In a study published in 2014, researchers found that sensitive caregiving in the first three years of life positively affects a person's social competence and academic achievement into adulthood. In fact, the impact on academic performance was stronger than the social impact. The results, which were based on scientists' study of about 240 people for their first 32 years of life, prompted the lead researcher to state this conclusion: "The study indicates that the quality of children's early caregiving experiences has an enduring and ongoing role in promoting successful social and academic development into the years of maturity."[4]

Just in case you're wondering, sensitive caregiving is defined as the extent to which a parent responds to a child's signals appropriately and promptly, is positively involved during interactions with the child, and provides a secure base for the child's exploration of the environment.[5]

That sounds like a nurturing mom to me! So you see, research continues to prove the all-around importance of good mothering. Moms, you have such an opportunity to enhance your children's intelligence and even social success. Your role is irreplaceable.

And of course, being involved in your child's education is going to be best for your child. Numerous studies prove this too.

- "Regardless of family income or background, students whose parents are involved in their schooling are more likely to have higher grades and test scores, attend school regularly, have better social skills, show improved behavior, and adapt well to school."[6]

- "The most accurate predictors of student achievement in school are not family income or social status, but the extent to which a student's family is able to (1) create a home environment that encourages learning; (2) communicate high, yet reasonable, expectations for the child's achievement and further career; and (3) become involved in the child's education at school."[7]

The Emotional/Psychological Realm of Nurturing

While providing superior educational opportunities is important, an even deeper level of need may remain unnurtured in the psychological or emotional realm of nurturing. Because many aspects of a child's identity exist internally, we parents often possess a blind spot when it comes to these "unseen" dimensions.

But unseen doesn't mean unimportant. Listen to what Erica Komisar had to say in 2016 about this dimension of nurturing. Komisar is a psychoanalyst and the author of *Being There: Why Prioritizing Motherhood in the First Three Years Matters*.

As a psychoanalyst and parent-guidance expert, I have seen society increasingly devalue mothering while idealizing work. At the same time, I have seen an epidemic of troubled children who are being diagnosed and medicated earlier and earlier with ADHD, early aggression and other behavioral and social disorders.

Many people say these two phenomena are utterly unrelated. I believe they are connected.

These disorders, I believe, are at least in part children's responses to stress in the environment and an inability to regulate emotional responses to it. In my clinical practice over the past 20 years, I have seen again and again ways that these disorders connect to the absence of mothers on a daily basis in children's lives.[8]

Komisar points to research on children's stress levels when Mom is not there and how that affects their brains. She then goes on to deliver this message: "The more emotionally and physically a mother can be present for a child in the first three years, the better the chance that child will be emotionally healthy and mentally well."[9]

Moms, we need to meet this emotional/psychological level of need. We can do so in so many ways. We can nurture our children emotionally and psychologically by the words we say to them and the messages we send them through our body language and our tone of voice. We can prevent or patch up emotional holes in our children's hearts through developing the art of nurturing. It takes a lot of unselfish creative work to do it right.

Let's talk about the heart. Both the physical and the emotional heart are unseen. Each needs to be fed, nurtured, and exercised to grow and function efficiently. Keeping each strong is essential.

When our awareness is heightened, we will find pleasure in doing those seemingly lesser things that, in fact, strengthen the child's inner being. Care of the emotional heart allows healthy fruit to be produced. What is flowing out of the heart at your house?

All of my boys have blessed and surprised me with special expressions of how they've felt cared for beyond the physical realm. Hopefully, letting you in on what one of my sons wrote while he was in college can help you understand the influence you're having on your little ones as you nurture them. Kent wrote,

> Over so many opportunities, you "chose" to be my mom first. Bless you for this, Mom! Please believe me, it has made all the difference. Mom, cheers to you for pouring yourself into me like you have. Thank you for loving me into the person I am and for a thousand special touches: for sending Dad my kiddie books in Vietnam so his taped voice could read to me, for French toast on game days, for being there at every game and every time I came home, for morning glimpses of you in the Scriptures, and for your constant affirmations. . . . Your love has endowed me with the confidence, the fearlessness, and the optimism that no kid should go without. You have certainly made some sacrifices to give me what I have, and I just want you to be reminded how much you are loved for all you do. Mom, I am so honored, humbled, and proud to be your son.

Making strong connections emotionally prevents possible "heart" failure later on in life.

The Spiritual Realm of Nurturing

Delving further, we reach the most important aspect of a child's development—a spiritual foundation. Without a relationship with Jesus Christ and following the design of the Creator who knows best, we live self-oriented lives without true wisdom or direction. Nurturing the spiritual dimension in our children is the most important job we could ever have.

Without a foundation, any house crumbles. Without spiritual development, our lives are not only incomplete but also destined for trouble, to put it mildly. When you follow the nurturing opportunities described in Deuteronomy 6:7 (when you walk by the way, when you lie down, and when you rise), you can help your children learn to know and live out the principles of God. Reading bedtime stories and praying together are two natural times to share spiritual tidbits. Driving your kids to the orthodontist, ball practices, or music lessons is a great time for conversation. Maybe you can offer spiritual direction while assembling a puzzle together or working on school projects.

Whenever our children mention fears or worries, we can point them to the ultimate comfort of Christ because we've had worries and have been comforted ourselves. One mother whose child had frequent bad dreams used the opportunity to pray with her child, asking for God's comfort and help in replacing the bad thoughts with good ones. Confidently and continually, the mother helped the child to stay in her own bed, teaching the child to trust and believe in God's watchful care. What an incredible opportunity we have when we are side by side with our children during this 20-year window of time.

When either a family member or a close friend dies, or something very traumatic happens in your family, displaying the strength of God through it all will help your kids mirror the same. When we seek refuge in God and His perspective, we show our kids how to trust a *very big God*. He can take us through this trauma. Life isn't easy: It's full of trouble, but we have a rock in our God. By nurturing their spiritual development, we give our children the tools to handle all of life.

A Nurturing Mom's Impact

Mom's Thousands of Actions	Lead to	Which Result in	Which Promotes
(continual active initiation of life boundaries*) demanding time, talent & energy	children feeling: ☐ important ☐ accepted ☐ cared for and formation of good: ☐ attitudes ☐ responses ☐ patterns	☐ emotional security ☐ positive self-esteem ☐ the enhancing of God's reputation ☐ the prevention of behavioral problems ☐ a healthy heritage	☐ A happy family ☐ Mom experiencing: pleasure hugs kisses smiles self-respect

(and exhaustion)

*Hebrew meaning of *train* in "train up a child" in Proverbs 22:6

Does Your Child Feel Nurtured?

Whenever I tried doing too many things when the kids were young, I felt their uneasiness, their sense of insecurity. Their responses reminded me to maintain that secure base at home and let go of some of my outside involvements, even though we desperately needed money that I could have earned. I didn't have all the research that I've shared so far in this book, but my maternal promptings convinced me to be more careful about nurturing my children.

It turns out that my maternal instincts are supported by additional scientific studies and discoveries that have been made since I was raising my children. There's even a new field of science called epigenetics, which has shown that cuddling and holding your baby affects your child on the molecular level![10]

Here's what Robert Winston, a British scientist, professor, and medical doctor, has to say about epigenetics and nurturing:

> Imagine if the hugs, lullabies and smiles from parents could inoculate babies against heartbreak, adolescent angst and even help them pass their exams decades later. Well, evidence from the new branch of science called epigenetics is reporting that this long-term emotional inoculation might be possible. . . .
>
> Parents can worry about things that just aren't important to their children's brain development and well-being such as giving them their own room,

buying them toys and taking them on expensive holidays. Instead, the most valuable gift that a child can receive is free; it's simply a parent's love, time and support. This is no empty sentiment; science is now showing why babies' brains need love more than anything else.

The new science of epigenetics is discovering more and more how our genes and our brains are affected by the lives we lead.[11]

Of course, God already knew all of this, and He gave moms their maternal instincts for a reason: so they would nurture their children. I realize that, for many reasons, not all women are mothers. But all women are born to nurture—it's who we are. In God's economy, the general plan is that women give birth to the babies. He has biologically created us so that when we give birth, the changes in our hormone levels promote bonding to our infants and our desire to care for and nurture our babies. As a beautiful feminine creature, you possess unique gifts to nurture. You have the ability to nurture; you just need to make sure your children are *feeling* nurtured.

When our children feel nurtured, it enables them to thrive and be secure. On the other hand, if they don't feel nurtured, they feel insecure. That sense of insecurity will lead them to pursue security through other, negative ways, such as alcohol, drugs, sex, pornography, or sexting, which in turn lead people to lie, cheat, steal, and do damage. So, then, we want to do everything possible to help our kids feel nurtured.

How do we do that? Before you become a mother, one of the best things you can do is develop your own healthy self-esteem. After we become mothers, we need to be sure that our self-esteem doesn't depend on our children. When we know who we are and seek guidance and reinforcement from the right places, we won't force our children into molds they were never designed to fill. That means not forcing them to look good because it will reflect well on us. Children gain power to be their best when we are free to give sacrificially of ourselves without stipulation or conditions. Sensing our fulfillment, they will model their own healthy self-esteem on ours. And they will feel nurtured.

Remember, your nurturing and giving have purpose. This quote from Anne Morrow Lindbergh lends insight when your tasks as a mom seem menial and never-ending; that's when you must remind yourself of your overall purpose to nurture your child well.

> Woman instinctively wants to give, yet resents
> giving herself in small pieces. . . . I believe that
> what woman resents is not so much giving herself
> in pieces as giving herself purposelessly. What
> we fear is not so much that our energy may be
> leaking away through small outlets as that it may
> be going "down the drain." . . . Purposeful giving
> is not as apt to deplete one's resources; it belongs

to that natural order of giving that seems to renew itself even in the act of depletion. The more one gives, the more one has to give—like milk in the breast.[12]

Many moms have good intentions and yet are simply unaware of the nuances of nurturing that take place in those emotional/psychological and spiritual realms. What might we be doing or not doing that gives our children negative feelings and thus negative behavior? It's good to do an evaluation from time to time.

The following chart will help you see at a glance the connection between a mom's actions and the feelings they invoke in her children.

Carefully read through the positive side of the chart and ask yourself how you're doing in each section. Ask yourself if your child is feeling nurtured. Are you doing the many things that will ensure a positive response from your child? Give yourself a pat on the back if you are doing these things well.

Then do the same evaluation as you carefully read through the negative side of the chart. Put yourself next to each of the actions listed. Does the action or attitude describe you? What about the child's responses on this side of the chart? Do you see that response in your child? If you see some issues, you now know where to make adjustments.

I'm begging you to please do yourself the favor of examining this chart very carefully. We speak the language of love

NURTURED OR NOT?

What Do the Children Feel?

Which is your profile?

P O S I T I V E

1. Nourishing, ensuring enrichment and closeness, equipping, giving creatively

The child feels: worthwhile, valued, loved, cared for

2. Promoting development of family root systems, child's trust, and boundaries; letting go

The child feels: secure, guided, confident

3. Tuning in to heart needs, honoring individuality, getting real, having a positive demeanor

The child feels: cared for, secure, wanted

4. Fostering, molding, training, rearing, giving what it takes, complimenting

The child feels: important, prepared, grateful, respected

5. Supporting by being available, listening, watching, feeling, sharing experiences, reaffirming, meeting unscheduled needs when load gets heavy and things are hard

The child feels: secure, important, accepted

6. Participating with enthusiasm, honoring, graciously hovering over the kids' life activities

The child feels: loved, valued, safe, emotionally prepared and supported

N E G A T I V E

1. Being distant, hoping for the best, assuming all is well

The child feels: overlooked, abandoned, uncared for, afraid

2. Discouraging children, offering no responsibilities and consequences, being too permissive or too domineering

The child feels: confused, wounded, insecure, emotionally scarred, betrayed, unstable

3. Being too busy, tired, stressed, divided, or selfish to attend to child's emotional needs; ignoring clues of child's pain and deviant behavior, being very negative about everything

The child feels: angry, rejected, resentful, indifferent, unimportant, depressed, poorly about self, apathetic, destructive

4. Continually demonstrating disapproval, leaving child with adult responsibilities (inappropriate for the age), giving child things instead of love, alienating the child

The child feels: abandoned, haunted by emptiness, disapproved of, rejected

5. Being absent continually (the child needs to make an appointment with the parent simply to ask a question)

The child feels: empty, sad, lonely, hopeless, isolated, explosive, plagued with abandonment

6. Being abusive

The child feels: trampled, afraid, desperate, powerless, shamed through the thousands of acts we do, and we speak the language of rejection through thousands of other types of actions as well. Be honest. Looking at yourself with new eyes through this evaluation can move you and your child into a better life.

A Complex Process

I am overwhelmed when I think of all the ways moms can make an impact.

While on an airplane, I ended up talking with the man next to me about nurturing. He noted how his neighbors had three children and yet they didn't take time to raise them. "My wife and I have only two children," he said, "but we spend time with them, helping them feel loved and cared for." Good observation.

Raising children does take time and effort. After caring for our young children during the long trip we made to Israel years ago, my mother-in-law said, "The true miracle in the biblical Sarah's life was not her conception during old age, but rather her ability to raise the child as an older woman." Caring for each realm simultaneously requires much energy.

It's a complex process that cannot be described easily. But with your inborn nature to nurture, your awareness of each realm, and God to guide you, you can use your gifts to nurture your children well. Remember, your ability to nurture makes good things happen. A nurturing mom's process creates an environment for a good harvest.

E-mails like the following from a friend's college son to his mom can remind us why our availability can make a difference. It just helps to be reminded of the difference we can make.

> What a blessing to be your son. Every aspect of my life has been shaped by your devotion. You have taught me that complaining is not justified no matter how bad the circumstances; you have taught me that life isn't lived best with the abundance of possessions. You have demonstrated perseverance and even long-suffering with a smile on your face. Mother, your sacrifice is evident to me in so many areas and will manifest itself as blessings in generations to come. The times growing up when you were *always* there to help me make the little decisions in life are not forgotten. For I have found that I now make the big decisions in my life through the template you established early on. Mother, I thank you for tireless devotion and endless sacrifice. I thank you for taking the struggles of life head on for us so that we might not be led astray.
>
> I thank you very much for giving of yourself for us. You have done a wonderful job. I couldn't have wished for a better mother. I love you.

May your children one day do as Proverbs 31:28 says: "Her children rise up and call her blessed."

CHAPTER 9

HOW CAN THE
SINGLE MOM DO IT?

MORE AND MORE MOMS are finding themselves handling all of the responsibility of raising a family. According to the US Census Bureau, out of about 12 million single-parent families in 2017 with children under age 18, more than 80 percent were headed by single mothers.[1] Today one in four children under age 18—a total of about 17.2 million—are being raised without a father.[2]

For most single mothers, that means working outside the home while parenting full-time. That's quite a load, to say the least.

From watching my single mother as I was growing up, and from witnessing the lives of many women who are in that situation now, four things stand out as essentials if you're going to succeed, not just survive, as a single mom.

1. Strive to have a positive attitude.

Attitude is everything. It affects both mental and physical health, and it largely determines whether you succeed or fail. People who think they can, usually can. People who don't think they can, usually can't—whatever the issue at hand, whatever the demand. You must have a positive attitude if you want to succeed. You can't be a victim in your mentality, continually ask "Why me?" and insist that others aren't taking care of you. Things are not easy as a single mom, no doubt about it—but you can make it with a positive attitude.

Single moms can become weighed down with emotions that are like strikes against them when it comes to choosing their attitude.

One strike can be anger. Anger because they're alone. Anger toward their ex-husbands. Anger because the world isn't fair. Anger because they have to struggle at a job and then go home and be both a mom and a dad to their children. Anger because people just don't understand the unrelenting demands that pull at them day in and day out, all week and all weekend.

When anger is unresolved, it causes damage inside and out. You don't have the time or money to let those damages derail you and make you unable to function at your job or with your kids. Just keep your mind on all the good things you can think of and what you're grateful for.

A second strike may be resentment. Unresolved anger can become resentment toward others. Very often it's misdirected and becomes aimed at parents, friends, or churches who may not have had a role in events or any power to sway them. Resentment hurts both the person who feels it and those around her.

If resentment isn't dealt with, it can turn inward and fester into bitterness. *Fester* is such an appropriate word. It's not used much anymore, but there was a time when any mother knew what festering was. Until recent improvements in medicines and sanitation, most people knew about boils. A boil is a painful, localized, pus-filled swelling of the skin. It's caused by a bacterial infection.

There's no real home treatment for a boil until it has formed a head—a channel to the skin's surface that eventually allows the pus to be drained off. When that appears, the wound can be lanced, drained, and cleaned. Then the swelling will go down and the boil can heal. If not drained, a boil will continue to generate pus, increasing the swelling, the pressure, and the pain. And the infection will spread, forming new boils.

Sometimes we feel as if we *deserve* to carry around bitter feelings. Letting go can feel like saying, "It really doesn't matter so much." But we feel just the opposite. It *does* matter so much. And it hurts so much. But not dealing with anger and resentment is like covering a boil, hoping it will simply go away. It won't. It will only fester, grow, spread, and erupt in other places. And the pain will only increase.

You don't really *deserve* to carry around your anger and bitterness. You *deserve* to be free. Letting go doesn't mean it didn't matter. It just means it isn't worth the cost of hanging on to the infection. Striving to have a positive attitude is like sunshine and fresh air. It's cleansing. It lightens our load. It strengthens and renews health. That's what you really deserve.

If you're locked up with bad feelings and damaged emotions and feel you can't move on, look for help. Almost always, unresolved issues will paralyze you emotionally. You need a source outside yourself to help you deal with those roadblocks, to sort them out, and to move beyond them. Smart people get help. Be smart. Confide in a close friend you can trust. Go to a pastor. Find a counselor. But get help.

Seeking the guidance of others isn't a show of weakness. It isn't just the latest approach in pop psychology. Such a wise approach to life has been known throughout the centuries. The biblical book of Proverbs (11:14, NASB) says, "Where there is no guidance the people fall, but in abundance of counselors there is victory."

With a positive attitude, you can take whatever situation you're in and make the most of it. It will be your greatest weapon in fighting despair. You can do it; you just have to believe you can.

Often it's not the circumstances so much as your view of them that needs the adjustment. Ruth Bell Graham tells a story of some fishermen in Scotland who gathered at an inn to rest and enjoy a cup of hot tea.

Just as the waitress was serving them, one of the men began describing the day's catch in typical fisherman gestures, and his right hand collided with a tea cup. The contents splashed all over the white-washed wall and an ugly brown stain emerged.

"I'm so terribly sorry," the fisherman apologized repeatedly.

"Never mind," said a man who jumped up from a nearby table. Pulling a crayon from his pocket, he began to sketch around the tea stain, and there emerged a magnificent royal stag with his antlers spread. The artist was Sir Edwin Henry Landseer, England's foremost painter of animals.

If an artist can do that with an ugly brown stain, what can God do with my sins and my mistakes if I give them over to Him?[3]

Julie is a young single mom and the sweetest person you could ever meet. You look at her and think, *The husband who abandoned her should have his head examined.* She didn't deserve that.

When her husband first left, Julie was overwhelmed with grief and the responsibility of caring for her two early-teen children alone. She struggled with feelings of rejection, fear, and devastation.

Her turning point toward renewed health and successful living came, she says, when she decided to lay aside her anger and despair and take positive responsibility for providing a secure home for her children. She knew it wouldn't be easy, but she was determined to do the job and do it well.

Julie realized she couldn't do the job alone, however, so she got involved with a support group through her church. From other members she learned coping skills and gained understanding. For her emotional health, she went to counseling and took classes. She even received training to help other women in the same situation.

It was difficult for Julie to quit blaming her former husband for her struggles and take this kind of responsibility. It required some heavy-duty anger resolution. But in the process, she became free to enjoy life again.

Julie works hard to provide a healthy environment for her kids, being there for them when she's not at her job, making financial sacrifices to give them opportunities for development—and all with a positive outlook on life. She has also found mentors to give them a constant, healthy male presence. She made the kids' daytime caregiver a friend of the family so she's not just "the sitter." And for the children's sake, she has tried to maintain as good a relationship as possible with their father.

Julie's life as a single mom takes extra effort day after day. But with determination and a positive attitude, she's making it.

The same can be true for you. Take heart. Strive to have a positive attitude. Get help in doing that if you need it. But begin to look at your situation in a different light, and make something of it that will count.

2. Refuse to give in to comparisons.

Comparisons can be toxic. First, they're usually shortsighted and incorrect. You never see the whole story. You don't know what other people may be dealing with. Anyway, we're each unique. None of us is alike, so why are we always comparing ourselves to one another?

When we make comparisons, we begin to have expectations. And often, those expectations are unreasonable. Just as a low-income family can't expect to have a house and car as nice as those of their more well-to-do neighbors, you can't expect to produce the same energy and creativity around the house as your married, stay-at-home friend next door. That's just not realistic. The best advice is to use your mental and physical energy in determining how to make the most of your situation, not focusing on comparisons or expending all your efforts trying to match someone else's standard of living.

A friend went flying in a small plane with his son. Something happened aboard the plane that caused it to go down. Our friend, Mick, survived. His son did not. As a result of his loss, he often says, "Things wouldn't be so hard if we didn't expect them to be so easy."

Things won't be so difficult for you as a single mom if you don't expect them to be easy. Refuse to make the comparisons. Refuse to buy into the expectations of keeping up with someone else, of having everything they have. The truth is, you won't be able to do everything. You may not have all you want or once had. But that's okay. Our lives are not measured in our abundance of things.

3. Never give up.

When you give up, you quit fighting. When you quit fighting, you lose. Never give up, because only by hanging in will you win.

My mom didn't give up. My dad had left our home, but for a while, he came back occasionally. Possibly the last time he did, Mom happened to get pregnant. You can imagine her thinking, *How will I be able to raise three children?* Yet she adjusted to her reality and continued on with her Christian outlook on life. That attitude and her dependence on God served her well, and she's been blessed for a lifetime by my younger brother, a pastor. Mom never gave up trusting her God.

Determination is necessary to overcome any obstacle, any challenge, any handicap. Whenever something doesn't work out, you have to try again. Maybe from a different angle, maybe in a different way, but you have to keep trying.

I used to play tennis with June. June had only one hand, so tennis was a big challenge for her. Imagine leaning to toss the ball in the air and then hit it with a racket, all using one hand. That's how she served. It wasn't easy. It took more energy than the normal way. But she never gave up, and she became an excellent player.

Another tennis partner battled cancer for 10 years before she died. Even during her chemotherapy, Marci never surrendered. It was months before I learned she wore a wig, one result of her treatment. It was not a big deal to her, nothing worth discussing.

She was determined not to miss a single week of tennis. One day she told me she had discovered why she had played so poorly the week before—she had a broken rib! I asked if she dared try to play again. "Oh, I'll be okay," she responded. "My ribs are taped this week." Marci simply refused to give up, and because of that, she enjoyed life despite the obstacles until the cancer finally won.

Both my friends had a plan, a focus. They set a goal in front of themselves, and they never gave up striving for it. Do the same for yourself. Set a goal, have a plan, and never give up.

4. Nurture your soul.

All of us need a resource outside ourselves. And everyone needs to go to that source for nourishment and refreshment. Nurture your soul. Refresh it. Don't neglect the needs of your innermost being.

For our family, our source was God Himself.

Back in that little migrant dwelling, my mother nurtured her soul from the Bible every day. When there was no soap for the washing machine, Mom would remind us that God would provide. When things were especially hard, she would rehearse for us how good God was, how He would never leave us. When my father became abusive and she was in physical danger, she would reflect on God's promises and remind us that He knows all things.

Imagine the inner strength she must have had to endure those hard days. That strength remained constant because she nurtured her soul. And imagine the foundation it gave her three children. We saw what really mattered. We saw how to lay a foundation to support us against anything we would ever face in life. We learned where to go for our own inner strength. And what security and emotional stamina that built into us!

My single mother lived through horrible circumstances with her abusive husband before he left (when I was a young teen), but she went on to live a victorious life. And her three kids not only survived, but thrived as well.

So, can the single mom do it? It's not an easy road. Strive to have a positive attitude. Refuse to give in to comparisons. Never give up. And nurture your soul. For Mom, that meant reading her Bible, believing *God was big enough* to deal with her problems, and then choosing to live like it. I pray these will be your resolutions too. They work!

CHAPTER 10

WHAT IS QUALITY CHILD CARE?

I KNOW YOU LOVE your children deeply and want to be the best mom you can possibly be. Because I want to be a friend who helps you toward that goal, I'm going to venture boldly into the child care topic and say what I believe with all my heart.

I realize that many moms reading this have children still at home and truly have no choice but to work outside the home. For you, it isn't just a matter of wanting to maintain a certain lifestyle or standard of living. But we need to discuss here the primary principle rather than focusing on exceptions to the rule of what's best for our kids. And remember, I grew up in a single-mom home, which means we kids didn't have her at home. Every mother must seek God's will for her unique situation. And every mother must pursue the best options possible for child care.

I know the facts: In 2016, 63 percent of mothers with children under age three were employed.[1] Those numbers have been pretty steady for more than a decade. As a result, child care is now a common part of many families.

Even so, for most of the rest of this chapter, I'm going to give my reasons for being leery of outside child care. Our choices are only as good as the information on which we base them. We need to become properly informed so we can make decisions based on solid facts rather than allowing our society to push us in a certain direction. Please read these pages in the spirit of loving concern with which they were written. And even if you have no choice but to work outside the home and leave your children in day care, please stay with me to the end, because there I will offer some suggestions for how to find the very best care.

First, let's consider how children are affected by early and long periods of separation from their mothers. British psychiatrist John Bowlby (who coined the term *attachment theory*) pointed out the deep psychological importance of the bond between a child and his mother: "'The young child's hunger for his mother's love and presence is as great as his hunger for food,' and . . . in consequence her absence inevitably generates 'a powerful sense of loss and anger.'"[2]

Psychologist Jay Belsky of Pennsylvania State University coauthored a report in 1979 concluding that day-care centers can be perfectly fine for young children. Eight years later in 1986, Belsky reversed his earlier position in a report published in the journal *Zero to Three*. He concluded that babies who spend more than 20 hours a week in non-maternal care during the first year of life risk having an "insecure attachment" to their mothers. Such children are more likely to become uncooperative and aggressive in early school years.[3]

In 2017, Erica Komisar wrote that she's seen the evidence of Belsky's conclusion in her own practice. Komisar, a psychoanalyst and parent-guidance expert who identifies herself as a mother first, writes that too many children in our society are undergoing stress because of separation from their mothers.

> Mothers serve two very important biological functions for children in the first three years. They soothe a child's distress in the moment, and they help regulate a child's emotions, not allowing them to go too high or too low. This lays down the foundation for resilience to stress going forward into adulthood. . . .
>
> When a mother or other primary caregiver is not present enough, a child experiences higher levels of stress. Research shows that when mothers and babies are separated, they both produce more cortisol, a stress hormone. The unrelieved production of cortisol may cause a baby or toddler

to become anxious and fearful, even when there's
no reason to be afraid. ADHD-like symptoms can
be a response to stress in the environment, just as
aggressive behavior can be a response to fear.[4]

The fact the US Centers for Disease Control and
Prevention reported a 400 percent increase since the 1980s in
people ages 12 to 19 on antidepressants and antianxiety med-
ications is no coincidence, Komisar said, as is the fact that
one in five children is now diagnosed with ADHD,[5] with a
42 percent increase in children diagnosed with ADHD from
2003 to 2012.[6]

It's interesting that despite labeling herself a feminist,
Komisar says it's the mother who needs to care for children
during those critical first three years when 85 percent of a
person's brain is developed.

Fathers and mothers are both critical to children's
development, but from a biological perspective, they
are not interchangeable. In the first three years, it is
particularly important for a baby's brain development
that they receive more sensitive nurturing. A mother
is more emotionally invested in her child. . . .
Other caregivers, even fathers, do not have the same
instincts.[7]

Research shows other negative impacts that too much
time in day care can have on children.

- In 2001, the longest-running child care study in the United States found that children who spent more time in non-maternal care during the first four and one-half years of life were more demanding, more aggressive, and more defiant than others, regardless of the type or quality of care, the family's socioeconomic status, or the sensitivity of the mother's parenting.[8]

- In 2005, that same National Institute of Child Health study reported that children "who had spent long hours in child care . . . still had poorer work habits and social skills" by the third grade.[9] At that time, a researcher on that study said, "Child care affects so many children that for society at large, even small effects are important. We have to consider whether we're creating a generation of children who have slightly less self-control, slightly more behavior problems."[10]

- In 2005, a study of 14,000 kindergarten children by researchers at Stanford and the University of California found that children from higher-income families had weaker social skills if they spent more than 30 hours a week in preschool, compared to children who were at home with a parent. The children's level of cooperation and sharing was lower.[11]

Does any mother want her child to have less self-control, more behavior problems, and poorer social skills? Does any mother want to risk a less-than-strong attachment to her child?

A friend took her car in to have the wheels balanced. After a short wait, the workman returned, filled out the paperwork, took her payment, and told her she was ready to go. But in his haste, he'd forgotten to replace the lug nuts on one wheel. Soon after she pulled onto a freeway, the wheel came loose and rolled across several lanes of traffic, causing a multi-car accident.

Sometimes things in life look fine, but then "the wheels fall off." Too much is at stake to take shortcuts, hope for the best, or assume someone else will do a good job.

Someone may have told you that a child naturally establishes strong bonds with a caregiver, and that's true. But that doesn't necessarily mean it's good. "A child's mind is like a video recorder, carefully transcribing every word, right down to the tone of voice and facial expressions. And all of it contributes to the person he will become. Some psychologists say his emotional pattern is set by the time he is two years old."[12]

And whom will the child mimic? The one with whom he spends significant waking hours. "A child needs at least one person he trusts and feels is in charge. That figure is the baby's 'touchstone'—the one he goes to when he is sick or frightened or sad. *All others are secondary*."[13] Attachment will take place. The question is, whom do we choose to take this influential position?

Whom will your child pattern himself after? Whom will he see when he wakes? When he experiences the rushes of good feelings from being fed, changed, or bathed, who will be indelibly etched in his mind, you or a caregiver?

Others just don't have the deep concern for my child that I have. No one else is ready to make the sacrifices, to take the time to nurture and encourage, that I am. So who could better care for my child, especially during his first years when he is so impressionable and easily molded?

Many people can carefully attend to your young child. Many people can provide quality food and supervision. But that doesn't ensure the emotional health, stability, or well-being of your little one. Mom, your child's identity will be indelibly stamped with the identity of the significant caregiver. His security and self-esteem will be permanently affected by his setting, especially if he has to establish himself in a crowd of other little folks all clamoring for attention, recognition, and regard.

You must look deeper than good food and supervision when you determine for yourself, "What is quality child care?"

And when you ask that question, know that poor child care in this country is common. Here's what a Georgetown psychology professor had to say in a Princeton University journal article about child care for infants and toddlers:

> In virtually all large-scale studies of child care in the United States, approximately 20% of the settings that participate in research have been found to fall below minimal thresholds of adequate care. These are settings in which caregivers more often ignore rather than respond to infants' and toddlers' bid for attention, age-appropriate or educational toys are

in scarce supply, and children spend much of their time alone in their cribs or wandering aimlessly—not engaged with adults, other children, or materials.

Even children in settings that exceed minimal thresholds of safety and quality do not necessarily experience care that is developmentally beneficial. . . . Studies showed that three-quarters of infant caregivers provided only minimal stimulation of cognitive and language development. . . .

Moreover, young children's needs for consistent caregivers often go unmet in this nation's child care settings. . . . This evidence explains why so many researchers who observe typical child care settings note that the majority of child care in the United States is no better than "mediocre."[14]

The bottom line is this: If you have to use child care, use it as a supplement to your nurturing, not a substitute. Treat your search for care with as much thoroughness as you would use in searching for the best heart surgeon. Use the following three guidelines in conducting your search.

First, look for a home atmosphere, with only one or two other children present at most, rather than a large-group setting like a franchised day-care center. There's just no way kids can get the individualized attention they need in the large-group situation. The ideal situation might be to find someone who can come to your home and give your children the most secure environment of all.

Second, do a thorough examination of all potential care-givers. Interview them closely, ask for references, and question all the references as well. It's not a bad idea to ask local churches for recommendations, but that's not foolproof, either. Examine those people as carefully as any others. And only consider people with a proven record of positive experiences.

Third, ask if you can spend some time in the day-care environment. As you observe a day-care provider, ask the same questions that researchers ask: "Does the caregiver respond quickly to the child's bids for attention or are they frequently ignored? Does she talk and read to the child a lot or just a little? Does she engage the child in age-appropriate activities and foster supportive friendships? Is she warm and affectionate or distant and harsh? Is she patient or easily over-whelmed by frustration?"[15]

Finally, look for caregiving situations that will allow you to maximize your own involvement with your children. Perhaps you can trade babysitting with a friend. You might find a job-sharing arrangement or a part-time position that meets your financial needs but doesn't require you to leave your children with someone else all day. Also explore the possibility of a home-based business if you have skills that can be used that way.

Mom, you have a unique place in your child's life, and you will make a unique impact—one way or the other. Make it the best within your powers to give.

CHAPTER 11

BUT WHAT ABOUT PERSONAL FULFILLMENT?

It GIVES ME GOOSE BUMPS to think that as adults, my children might recall words of wisdom that I shared with them in their younger years. Those tidbits shared just might move them out of a dark season and into a place of knowing how to handle a difficult situation.

That's what happened to the singer-songwriter Paul McCartney. His mother died when he was 14, but when he was going through a difficult time many years later, her words, "Let it be," comforted him.[1] The song he wrote because of his mother's inspiring words became known to millions. The famous Beatle talked about that night in a 2013 newspaper article, saying that if he had a time machine, he would want to "go back and spend time with [his] mum."

One night, somewhere between deep sleep and insomnia, I had the most comforting dream about my mother. . . . So in this dream twelve years later, my mother appeared, and there was her face, completely clear, particularly her eyes, and she said to me very gently, very reassuringly: "Let it be." It was lovely. I woke up with a great feeling. It was really like she had visited me at this very difficult point in my life.[2]

Just as Paul McCartney's mother Mary spoke words of wisdom to him, you, too, have the opportunity to share words of wisdom with your children that will echo in their minds. Mom, you are handed an influential platform in life to fill your children's reservoirs with the way they should go (see Proverbs 22:6). As the Lord instructs in Deuteronomy 6:6-7, the character and intentions of our Creator God shall be on our hearts, and we are to "teach them diligently" at all times, as routinely as breathing, so that proverbially (Proverbs 22:6) when our children are old they "will not depart from it."

You have the incredible power to train your children's subconscious minds and fill them with discerning answers to life's problems. They will not need to flounder if you have imparted the wisdom from life's instruction book, from the ultimate authority of how life works best. As moms, we can experience personal fulfillment by equipping our kids with the answers to life's ongoing questions. And then, at needed moments, they will have instant recall to those answers.

Even though providing this type of foundation for life is a high calling, we fail to see motherhood respected in our culture. Television doesn't seem to know how to portray moms. Unfortunately, so many times we see women being encouraged to assert their intelligence and influence everywhere but in the home. I could tell many stories of how my talented daughters-in-law have given themselves to their children in the home, while being employed part-time as well. Yet they were not encouraged to work only part-time by our culture. As our daughter-in-law Jami Lyn was graduating from college summa cum laude, she was actually told not to "waste" her life "just" being a mother. (She and our son Blake now have two children.)

Many women have acted as if motherhood were a brand of mediocrity to bear—if you can't make it in "the real world," you can always fall back on being a mother, but you'll have to live with the stigma. But now we see these women, with their biological clocks running down, going to unbelievable lengths to do what they've always shown disregard for—being a mother.

During a break at a conference at which I spoke, a woman approached who had been reading ahead in the program schedule. She didn't like what she saw coming, and she told me there were things she wanted me to omit—things like the importance of mothering, raising kids, and making the family a priority.

She didn't want to hear anything about staying at home. She didn't want to hear anything about having kids. And she didn't want anyone making her feel guilty. She was a professor at a local university, and she wanted to stay in the classroom where she deserved to be.

I tried to explain graciously that what I would be presenting was generally applicable (after all, having kids is the only way to ensure future generations) and that I wouldn't have time to address all the exceptions. Since I was the speaker and already had my presentation prepared, and since I happened to believe in my message and intended to share it anyway, she walked away in a huff.

After the break, as I stood to continue my talk, I saw her standing by the back door. She never left, but she never returned to her seat, either. I guess she was stationed near an escape route in case the pressure became too much. How sad to have made a decision and yet to feel so greatly intimidated by it.

She'll probably never change her mind. Maybe that's best. Maybe not. You may feel much the same. Or you may be confused, not knowing which route to take.

Let me offer an example of a friend who changed her mind about mothering. My two older sons both had her as a teacher in high school. When they knew her, she was single and adamant about never having children. She once told her class, "If a baby fell out of the sky and landed in my lap, I wouldn't have an inkling of what to do with it."

Years later, I saw her at a ball game. She laughed as she told me, "You'll have to tell the boys to drop by the house when they're home from college. It's been an amazing transformation. They'll have to see it to believe it." She's a very fulfilled mother and wouldn't trade her children for the world. You'd never know she was the same person.

When she learned I was writing a book about mother-hood, she wrote this to me:

"I don't ever want to have kids!"

I wonder how many times in my life I've said those words? Hundreds probably. And I really meant it. If there was ever anyone who was sure about not having children, it was me!

Now here I sit, a 37-year-old mother of a 6-month-old baby, and I laugh as those words echo in my memory! Describing what my son means to me is an impossible task. I could never put down in words the feelings I have when I'm doing all those things mothers do, feeding him, changing him, comforting him, playing with him, holding him, or watching him sleep.

The joy I get from taking care of this helpless little human being and knowing that I'm there for him when he needs me is immeasurable! He's such a precious little one. I can't imagine my life without him. He's added a different dimension to who I am. He's helped me to focus on someone other than myself, in the process making me a more caring person, I think, toward everyone else in my life.

I still work. I love my job teaching high-school English, and I always will. But I've cut back my schedule, and now I only teach part-time. Instead of being the sole fulfillment in my life, as it was for so many years, now it's only a part of my life. Real living begins when I pick up my baby after school and head home to be a mom. I'm a changed person, and I love it!

All the people in my life who heard me for so many years say I didn't want kids would be proud of me. Being a mother is the best choice I ever made. Motherhood is terrific!

Christian author and speaker Elisabeth Elliot quotes a mother, Brenda Sawyer, who says, "I can't think of another career more challenging and satisfying than to pour my energies into the daily task of making order out of chaos, music out of noise, communication out of babble, purposefulness out of purposelessness, pointing chubby little wayward feet gently toward the Path, lighting ignorance with knowledge and confusion with understanding."[3]

Another good example is Dr. Mary Ann Froehlich. She holds a "doctorate in music education/music therapy from the University of Southern California, an MA degree in Theology (pastoral care) from Fuller Theological Seminary, and MA and BM degrees in piano and harp performance and music therapy.

"She is also a certified child life specialist and has published her dissertation research on the use of music therapy with chronically and terminally ill children.

"A Suzuki music educator and Registered Music Therapist—Board Certified, Mary Ann has worked in hospitals, schools, churches, and private practice. She is a frequent contributor to professional journals. Her piano/harp arrangements [have been published as well]."[4]

And her attitude toward mothering?

When I was working and in graduate school, more than one person asked me why I was working so hard. Wasn't it all going to be wasted when I stopped to have a family? Why didn't I stop to have children now and get it over with, and pursue my career later? They made motherhood sound like a prison term, a bad pill to swallow, a time for putting life on hold. Raising a family was posed as the antithesis of growing, learning, thinking, and contributing a specialization.

I have found family life to be quite the opposite. Not only is this the most enjoyable time of my life, but my children are also the most stimulating and challenging teachers I've had yet, and they have tapped every resource in my background.[5]

Those women use strong words describing their experience as mothers: "immeasurable, precious, a new dimension, real living, terrific, nothing more challenging and satisfying, the most enjoyable time of my life, stimulating." Does that sound like a stigma to bear? Does that sound like wasted, unfulfilled living?

Don't listen only to the call of the politically correct, who tell you to lean in to your career and make something of yourself. Sure, you have rights to be your own person. But your children have rights too. Among them is the right to be properly nurtured and given a strong foundation upon which to build their lives.

Over the years, I've received many letters from mothers who had gained a new perspective about the worth of being a mom, telling me of a fulfillment they hadn't thought possible. One doctor wrote me five years after reading the first edition of this book, saying she was so content with the motherhood role that she doubted she would return to medicine. I simply suggest that there are different seasons in life, and you can put creativity to use in each season.

Yes, some women cannot become mothers. Others have lost their children. Some simply have not felt adequate or gifted for the task and have avoided it. I have no criticism to aim at them.

I do take exception, though, to those who bad-mouth and denounce motherhood. How arrogant!

Do they think they were produced by a 3-D copier? Are they really unaware that many of the personal strengths they now flaunt, they owe to their mothers, either through inherited genes or acquired skills at the feet of or thanks to the efforts of their mothers?

Motherhood is not an entry-level service position for mindless, insecure, second-class citizens. It is the noblest of callings. To be entrusted with the very life, health, and well-being of a tiny human person is a great gift and honor. To realize this small child reflects traits and characteristics of you, your spouse, and your families is a mind-shattering and heartrending realization. To invest your time and best efforts into a child and to watch him grow, develop, and excel is to be part of the creative majesty of life itself.

People talk about a bucket list of what they wish to do or accomplish in their lifetimes. For me, the thrust of any bucket list is to make a difference with my life. So, then, I have personal fulfillment in knowing I've worked to provide an unmistakable biblical standard—such that creates a joyful, purpose-driven life for the kids God gave me as Mom.

I would guess that Barbara Bush, who cherished her role as a mother, was personally fulfilled. After the former first lady's death in 2018, her graduation speech to the Wellesley class of 1990 made the news again. This mother of six children, 14 grandchildren, and seven great-grandchildren shared some wise words with that career-minded audience:

"At the end of your life, you will never regret not having passed one more test, not winning one more verdict or not closing one more deal. You will regret time not spent with a husband, a child, a friend or a parent. . . . Whatever the era, whatever the times, one thing will never change: Fathers and mothers, if you have children—they must come first."[6]

At Bush's funeral, six of her granddaughters each read

a section from Proverbs 31, beginning with the line "Her children rise up and call her happy; her husband too, and he praises her: 'Many women have done excellently, but you surpass them all.'"[7]

Never let anyone denounce motherhood or dissuade you from experiencing it. May you truly enjoy and feel personally fulfilled by the difference you can make as a mom. As the ladies in this chapter have told you, it transcends all other experiences.

CHAPTER 12

WHAT DO YOU SAY TO THE WORKING MOM?

IF I'M CONVINCED of anything, it's that there is one non-negotiable in the discussion of working moms—the welfare of our children. If we're sacrificing that, we're making a terrible mistake. We must do all we can to develop the hearts and spirits of our children. Beyond that, though, there are probably fewer black-and-white answers than we might like.

I've expressed repeatedly my strong belief that I needed to be home with my three active boys when they were little. I was convinced then that I was doing the right thing, and I believe it still.

But much—very much—has to do with the circumstances, the season of life, and the personalities within your family. What may be best in one home might be quite different in another.

In our situation, I have been at one point a stay-at-home mother, and I feel it was the best thing I could have done. I strongly recommend it when your children are young. I think it is very important for their development. At another season, I've been a part-time working mother, I've enjoyed it, and I had a clear conscience that it did not harm my boys. But even then, I couldn't simply change my focus away from mothering, assuming the kids were old enough that it wouldn't affect them.

If you're considering a job outside the home, I would encourage you, *work in addition to mothering, never in lieu of mothering.*

Children have different needs at different ages. Mothers have different levels of talent, strength, and capacity to meet those needs. Husbands have different levels of expertise, understanding, and availability. Every family is unique, and even within each family, needs change with different seasons of life. *So we should be less concerned about having the right answers and more concerned about meeting the right needs.*

My friend Sharon sets the stage well to begin this discussion:

Rather than discussing the issue of working or not working outside the home, we need to address the issue of nurturing those in our homes—both our husbands and our children. When we address that issue, all the incidentals will fall into place.

"Career women" and "working women" are not synonymous—yet many times that's how it's portrayed. Mothers can work outside the home without being preoccupied with their careers to the detriment of their families.

At the same time, "stay-at-home moms" and "nurturing moms" are not synonymous, either—yet that's how they're often portrayed as well. I have friends who looked forward to the day their children were born and now look forward to the day they're gone. The only time they seem to enjoy them in the interim is when they perform to their liking. Being a stay-at-home mom *doesn't mean you'll automatically be a nurturing mom.*

The truth is, stereotypes just don't work. And being at home is not the goal. Making the biggest impact in your home is the goal. Though proximity is critically important, we cannot assume that our proximity alone will automatically ensure success. Being around and being attentive are both needed. Some mothers stay at home and yet have, to a degree, emotionally abandoned their children. You can picture many moms staying on their smartphones all the time and paying absolutely no attention to their children, despite their being in the home.

What's more, there are no guarantees, even if you do

all the right things. Many good parents have experienced great disappointment with children who seemed to have had the right environment and yet made all the wrong decisions. Children are not robots; they get to choose what they will do. We all know those who go the route of being the prodigal. Some come back, some don't, and some sooner than later.

The real objective is to make good decisions as parents based on a realistic evaluation of your family's needs.

Can we have any career we desire and at the same time be the kind of nurturing mother we want to be?

Mary Louise Kelly, a journalist, author, and mother of two, learned that she could not, and spoke about it on a 2013 National Public Radio broadcast. She was working as NPR's Pentagon correspondent when she had this realization.

> I was covering the Pentagon and that meant traveling with the [US] Defense secretary. And on this particular day, we were in Baghdad . . . trying to get across the city in Black Hawks. . . . We were about to take off, we're all in flak jackets and helmets, and my phone rang and I'm yelling, trying to hear it, as the helicopters are gearing up. And it was the school nurse at my youngest son's school saying he's really sick, come get him. And I said, well, I can't. I'm in Bag . . .
>
> And she interrupted me and said no I mean he's having trouble breathing. We need to get him . . .

to the hospital, now. Can you come get him? And
as I was trying to answer, the line went dead and the
helicopter took off. . . . It was . . . crystal clear . . .
the work I want to do and the mom I want to be,
they are not simpatico.[1]

A woman can have it all—just not all at once. I believe a
woman can have a successful career. I believe a woman can be
a very good mother. I even believe a woman can work outside
the home and be a good mother.

Yet we all have only 24 hours in a day, so there are physical
limitations to what we can accomplish in that time period
in addition to meeting our children's emotional needs. Our
decision of what is essentially important for today's list is
made every day by how we live our lives. Some can accomplish more than others—it's just a fact of life.

Working at a job outside the home and being completely
focused on a career are two different things in my mind.
Sometimes work is necessary, as it was for my mom. Sharon
also felt she had little choice about working.

One of the reasons I went back to work was that
it was either Dennis adding another job or me
picking up part-time work. It wasn't because we were
trying to move up the financial ladder—we were
just in a critical stage. We felt very strongly that the
added hours of a second job for Dennis would be
detrimental to his relationship with his children. We

even discussed this with the kids at the time, and
they wanted me to work part-time—they didn't want
to give up more time with their dad.

Now she works a part-time, flexible schedule, more to
make a positive impact in her community than for the sake of
family finances. She's just geared to run the race at a fast pace.
The challenge and the accomplishments of her job bring her
great satisfaction.

But there is a danger we need to be alert to—allowing work
to get ahead of the nurturing. In her book *Can Motherhood
Survive?* Connie Marshner writes, "All of Western civilization
. . . is being enveloped by a miasma of anti-motherhood, and
few of us can escape its effects. . . . I made some very serious
mistakes when I was a career-centered mother, and I know
that plenty of other mothers, even well-intentioned Christian
mothers, are repeating the very same mistakes today."[2]

There's the warning flag again—she was a "career-centered
mother" making "serious mistakes" in raising her kids. We
should heed her warning.

My son Kent wrote to me of a woman in one of his psychology classes who cried as she told the class of her career mind-set
when her kids were little. They never enjoyed extracurricular
activities after school because there was no one there to shuttle
them back and forth. They missed out on those experiences,
and they still feel the loss. She regrets her choices and has had
to deal with the consequences. Even today, she isn't included
in her kids' lives the way she'd like to be. Yesterday, she was

too busy for them. Today, following in her footsteps, they've become too busy for her. They aren't responding to the fact that she worked, but to the fact that, in their minds, her work became more important than they were.

Helen Hayes MacArthur, the first lady of the American theater, enjoyed a great deal of success as an actress. But later in life, she admitted she wished she had spent more time with her family. "For all the deep satisfaction it gave me," she said, "my career was not a good thing for us [her husband and herself] or the children."[3]

Let's keep in mind that a successful balancing of work and motherhood requires more than just planning your day carefully. Consider the lawyer who gave birth to her first child a few years after making partner at her firm, and then tried being a mom and doing her job. As she told the *Atlantic* in 2016, "Something's gotta give. I can't give 100 percent to everything."[4]

> Even though she believes the firm would have
> allowed her to work part-time and still retain her
> partner status, she says she couldn't imagine not being
> available to her clients around the clock; nor could
> she imagine letting anyone else take care of her child
> during the day. She walked into her supervisor's office
> . . . and delivered her resignation.[5]

A Wall Street financial planner (and expectant mother) left her job and tried to earn a master's in a field that would allow more flexibility. But she soon learned that there's only so much time in the day.

"I was studying for an exam at the library, and making a grocery list at the same time," she recounted. "I couldn't handle it." Now a stay-at-home mom of three kids, she said she doesn't see how she and her husband could "logistically" run their household if she took a job, since he works long hours and travels often.[6]

What a tragedy to rationalize or buy into the message that you can do it all and that you deserve it, and then to find you've come up short at the expense of those you love most. Let's make sure we're finding a balance—not a compromise where both sides lose, but a balance where we can do one thing well without taking away from the more important thing that *must* be done well.

Years ago, we invited several church leaders and their wives to our home for a formal dinner. I had worked hard all week to prepare a gourmet meal. I had rehearsed each step, every recipe. This was going to be a pleasurable experience, an evening they would not forget.

I wanted to be a good hostess as my guests arrived, and I purposely took time to enjoy conversation with each of them. After appetizers and some small talk, everyone stepped to the table to find his or her place.

As I prepared to serve our guests, I realized the soup I had made had burned. All my special ingredients were lost. I actually had to throw it out. I hadn't been there stirring it as the recipe instructed.

Earlier that day, I'd driven 50 miles round-trip to buy dinner rolls from a certain restaurant. I opened my oven door to find that they, too, had burned while I had been preoccupied with my guests. Even the main course of my gourmet dinner was a disaster. I hadn't timed it right.

I had planned well. I had purchased all the right ingredients. I had done my best. I simply wasn't able to do all the things called for that night. I couldn't be in two places at once.

The experience taught me I couldn't be in two places at once in life, either. And my caution to you is simple: Don't push too hard. Don't try to take on too much. You might see others who seem to pack 48 hours into 24. They don't. Yes, some are much faster than others. Some of you can accomplish a great deal. But don't assume you can be in two places at once. Don't think you can pack 48 hours into 24. It's a lie.

You've heard this before. A two-quart saucepan holds just two quarts, no matter how much you pour into it. Something is being lost over the edge if you try to pour in more. People can't keep cramming more into their lives, either. Something is being ignored, omitted, or lost. I'm as guilty as any of you.

Know your capacity. Keep your priorities well in mind. Then go ahead and work if it will be rewarding to you. Just don't work at the expense of your children.

One last caution. Some may assume that if you can't be in two places at once, simply do two things at one time. Here, too, approach it wisely, and don't make ambitious commitments.

Since I was a pastor's wife, it was inevitable that individuals would seek me out for advice and counsel. When the church was small and our older boys were young, probably two and four, I did a great deal of counseling over the phone. It seemed the perfect thing to do; I could help people and still be at home.

But when people express their deepest fears and concerns, you have to keep your full attention on them. You can't have noise surrounding you. You can't be interrupted with questions and requests. You need to be left alone to concentrate. And you never know when a call is going to come or how long it will last.

This ministry of mine frustrated the boys more than I realized. One day, one of them got my attention. We had an old upright piano that was a prized family possession. One of the wooden knobs on the keyboard cover had a screw that had stripped. It would sit in place for appearance's sake, but if you pulled on it, it would come right out. On that fateful day, one of my boys, weary of being shushed and shooed again, took his frustrations out on my prize. He pulled the wooden knob from its cradle and used the exposed screw to scribble all over the wooden front. I got the message.

Those scars in the finish remain to this day. They remind me of my careless inattention to their needs. I thought my proximity ensured my success. I didn't give much attention to this season of the boys' lives and their particular needs. For me, the consequences were only scars on my piano. I saw my mistake and changed. Thank heaven those were the only scars caused by my inattention. Interestingly enough, that piano is now in that son's home, where it can forever remind him of that life lesson years ago, for a new generation to heed.

What do I say to a working mother? Don't feel guilty if you have to work, or even if you just *want* to work, as long as your work is a balance, not a compromise; thought through, not a rationalization. Reconsider if you think you can pursue a full-time career and be a truly successful mother at the same time. You can probably have it all. Just don't try to have it all at once. Your children will be with you so few years. Focus on them and make work secondary. After they're gone, you'll have a different season of life.

CHAPTER 13

WHAT DO YOU DO WHEN YOUR WORLD FALLS APART?

SOMETIMES LIFE IS HARD. Sometimes being a mother is hard too—maybe even overwhelming. Having minimum energy to "keep on keeping on" with little sleep might even be the least of your concerns, as hard as that is. You may have had crises and disasters come so unexpectedly, and they may have so devastated you that you ask, "What about me? What am I to do? I can't take your advice. It's too late. What you warned of has already happened—all of it and much more."

Or you may say, "You didn't say anything about those catastrophes we have no influence over—medical problems, handicaps, large inequities, violations, marriage conflicts, deaths, financial disasters, job losses. How in the world am I to face such problems when I have no power to influence or correct them?"

In short, you may feel as if your world has fallen apart and there's nothing you can do to put it back together. Perhaps not because of past events but present circumstances, you feel life will never be normal again, and you're having trouble holding on.

I've thought a lot about the issues many of my friends face every day. Overwhelming, paralyzing issues. I couldn't begin to address them all. And if I tried, I wouldn't do them justice. But as I've turned those problems over in my mind—categorizing them, weighing them, looking for encouragement—several approaches have come to mind that I think bear consideration.

Finding solutions is never simple, and when you do find them, working them out is seldom easy. But regardless of what you face, Mom, I believe the 10 suggestions that follow can give you hope and bring you strength. Don't discount them quickly. Don't brush them off because an illustration doesn't match your circumstances. Pain paralyzes, and you're too special to be held captive under the weight of pain you may be bearing.

So look for the application to your circumstance. Imagine how you could use each suggestion actively to your advantage. In the process, remember you are that mirror we mentioned before that is reflecting to your children how to handle the traumas we face.

1. Never give up.

"Never give up" is the first advice I give single mothers. As long as you're trying, you're winning. Only when you give up do you lose.

That doesn't mean you have to overcome every obstacle. It doesn't mean you have to win the battle today or tomorrow or even this year. It just means you will always commit yourself to taking one more step. (Any possible chip on your shoulder here won't work.)

It doesn't mean you never take a break, either. Taking a break from your circumstance or your surroundings is not only a temporary relief, but it can help you gain perspective as well.

Instead, it means never saying, "I can't handle this anymore, and I won't try." How can you know how close you might be to that breakthrough? How can you know how near you are to finally seeing things in a new light that will give you the strength and determination to deal with the situation? How can you know how close help may be?

If you think you can, you probably can—no matter the issue at hand. If you think you can't, you probably can't. Never giving up is saying, "I think I can." No matter how small you feel your chances are of succeeding, you know you have no chance if you give up. And if you know you've been raised with a "normal" pattern of being negative, you can choose a "new normal."

So beware as you decide how to proceed with your hardship.

If you find your strength waning as you compare yourself with "successful" moms around you, remember that comparisons are toxic. Those moms are real people too. Everyone has her own problems and obstacles to overcome. You just don't see the deep water she may have come through. Successful people aren't those who have never faced dilemmas. They're the ones who never gave up despite the dilemmas. They've done battle. And that can be you, too.

2. Grieve your loss.

You may have experienced great loss in a number of ways. You may not even fully realize all the losses you've faced. Loss can be material, relational, or perceptional. The way your physical body functions may have been significantly altered. Your role in life may have changed dramatically.

When loss does occur, a process called *grief* needs to happen for recovery to take place. And that may require some outside assistance. Many churches have classes that can be helpful with grief.

Please don't confuse pressing on through pain with pushing it away—out of sight, out of mind, out of reach. We have to deal with it, to go through a process of coming to terms with the situation and growing beyond it. But that's too much of a process to adequately develop within the confines of this book.

Basically, you must face what has happened and identify the loss. You must acknowledge your feelings and admit to and submit to the pain you've tried to deny or hold back.

These steps will enable you to discover new insights into what has taken place and how to apply what you've learned to the process of moving on.

Progressing from what was to what is requires unlearning old patterns and learning new ones—new ways of life, new states of mind. It also takes perseverance and time, but with liberal doses of both, you will grow.

I have two dear friends who both suffered the loss of their husbands and sons within a short period. As a result, they've learned a lot about this process firsthand. One of them, Jackie, now helps others work through their grief. She always encourages them to allow themselves to go through the process rather than deny it, to let their hearts feel and process the pain. Stuffing your feelings doesn't make them go away. It just shoves them below the surface, where they can fester unattended.

Grieving your loss will help you gain perspective and show you how to heal. It will help you accept responsibility for moving on. And it will help you release your anger and forgive instead of thrusting your anger on undeserving family and friends.

And never grieve alone. Search out a friend who will help you, someone you can trust. Work through it, and don't deny it. You'll be better off.

3. Get help.
Whether for lack of direction, pride, or confusion, we're often slow to get help. But we're frequently in desperate need

of another perspective, special insight, or specific training to help us through crises so we can move on.

Mom, maybe you're in deep pain, and you just need a trusted friend who will listen, who will be there, and who will walk with you through the pain. Isolation will only hinder your recovery. If a friend can't help, look for a support group where you can find encouragement and understanding.

Maybe you have needs that require special resources—it could be relief help with a child who has special needs. It could be equipment to deal with a medical condition.

Maybe you have concerns that are paralyzing you or past hurts that plague you that need to be explored. Perhaps you need a professional to guide you. There's no way you can be capable of meeting all your own needs or sorting out all your own problems. And don't allow anyone to make you feel there's shame in seeking wise counsel. Avoiding counsel may only prevent you from enjoying a more fulfilled life.

Focus on the Family offers a onetime complimentary counseling consultation from a Christian perspective, as well as referrals for licensed Christian counselors in your area. To reach Focus on the Family's counseling service by phone, call 1-855-771-4357 weekdays 6:00 a.m. to 8:00 p.m. (mountain time).

Maybe your crisis requires the kind of help that will cost money, but you're reluctant to commit yourself. If you need help, however, do what you must to find it. Financial assistance is often available. The bottom line: Smart people get help. Proverbs 24:5-6 says, "A man of knowledge enhances his might . . . and in abundance of counselors there is victory."

4. Cherish your relationships.

Problems have a way of isolating us from others. Just when we most need those we care about, we often feel least willing to be with them. What a paradox!

Don't cut yourself off. Don't destroy relationships through neglect or rejection. Isolation can be one of the most devastating aspects of any crisis. Don't cut off lifelines in your time of greatest need. If anything, give extra nourishment to those relationships. Take time to reflect on their importance and cherish them. There's a Turkish proverb that says, "No road is long with good company."

5. Admit your failures—and then move on.

We can cause ourselves a great deal of insecurity and distress by trying to avoid looking at ourselves realistically, refusing to admit any blame or failure. Avoiding failure won't make it go away; it will just make it loom larger.

We all make mistakes, but too many of us refuse to admit them. It's too threatening to look in the mirror and see our errors. It seems easier to deny them and move on. But nothing changes when we deny making mistakes. We don't learn. We don't adjust. We don't correct our course.

None of us can foresee the future. Few of us can see the present all that clearly. Often that's why we find ourselves not knowing what hit us. But when the dilemma has our attention, that's the best time to look at it realistically, to see what went wrong, and to learn how to avoid having it happen again.

All of us need to analyze our particular circumstances. After we've considered where we might have failed, we need to learn from it, chalk it up to experience, set it aside, and move on.

6. Keep loving.

Sometimes we're not the ones who bring on the crisis. Maybe your children have caused you pain by their actions, their choices, or their lifestyles.

Disapprove foolish choices, but don't reject the child who made them. The loss you incur by doing that will only add to your pain. It won't help it. It won't justify it. It won't heal it. It will only intensify it.

Love is the one commodity we always have enough of. It's the only thing in life that is not diminished by being divided and shared. It's the only thing we have the freedom to give away lavishly. No matter how much love we give, we'll never run out. We'll never find there's too little left to share.

And most of all, love is the most certain healer—of you, of the situation, of the others involved. Make sure it's spontaneous. Make sure it's unconditional—especially when it's least deserved. That's what makes love different. Real love is often given despite the circumstances. It's acceptance when someone isn't acceptable. And that's when we all need it most. I think you'll find plenty of situations where that applies, don't you?

7. Don't dominate.

It's easy, in crises, to either be overwhelmed and paralyzed or to try to take control. Sometimes taking control of a situation is exactly what you should do—if you're supposed to be the one in charge. But it's not good if you're trying to "fix" the people involved. A domineering mother tends to do that, to try to manipulate people into acting the way she thinks is best.

A domineering mother can be one of the most dangerous and damaging parts of any crisis. That negative influence probably accounts for as many disorders as any other factor in the lives of children. Unfortunately, many such mothers don't have a clue that they are part of a problem.

I've seen a number of homes where Mom had wanted her child to be a certain sex. When she didn't get what she wanted, she directed that child's life, possibly subconsciously, into shaping that child to be the little girl or little boy she preferred. The consequences were devastating. My own father's mother fit this category. Unfortunately she caused a whopping load of dysfunctions to be seeded in my father's world. Mom, don't dominate your family and sow the seed of unpleasant and devastating fruit.

8. Be creative.

When we're stuck in bad situations and seem powerless to break free, it's because we continue to see the situation in the same light and see the same obstacles as overwhelming. When we bring creativity to a situation, we can begin to see it from a different angle, and we can think of new solutions or ways of handling the problems day to day. Go down a different alley instead of staying in the same one and getting mugged.

When plan A doesn't work, go to plan B, and if plan B doesn't work, keep going all the way through the alphabet. If necessary, start again with plan AA. You just have to get creative by choice—don't let yourself have a victim's mind-set.

Mom, it may be little more than your monotonous schedule that has you frustrated. Don't allow yourself to get bogged down because you don't have the energy to change. Don't let the lack of funds, painful experiences, or other handicaps cause you to live under a low-hanging black cloud.

Move, Mom, move! Creativity never blossomed in the midst of comfort and ease. It's stimulated by need. If you have need, channel that energy into finding solutions. Think about it. You're more creative than you realize. You just have to apply yourself. It takes the right attitude, and it takes action. Once you get started, you might be surprised where it will take you.

Creativity often opens the door to changes that can amaze and refresh us. There's always a way to lighten the load. And once again, don't be afraid to ask for help.

9. Let the process refine you.

Heat both melts butter and hardens steel. The effect depends on what a substance is made of. Fire can either destroy or purify.

Shaun is severely afflicted with cerebral palsy. When he was born, his parents, Terry and Cheryl, were faced with a myriad of decisions. Probably the least obvious at the time, but the most critical over the long haul, was the decision of whether they would allow Shaun's condition to destroy them or refine them.

But Terry and Cheryl made a lot of good decisions. And the most important was that choice not to let the stress resulting from Shaun's condition ruin them or their marriage. From the moment of his birth, they knew what they had to do. As Terry said, "He's our son, and we'll love him no matter what."

Life hasn't been easy since they made that decision. Loving hasn't been easy, either. They've learned that love is giving yourself unselfishly to another. Through the years of interrupted sleep, constant care, and the never-ending routine of accomplishing even the most basic tasks, they've matured. There hasn't been much room for selfishness or self-pity. There has been too much to do. But instead of their sacrifice making them less, it has made them more—more loving, more compassionate, more faithful. It has built their character and refined their marriage. Cheryl confided to me,

Sometimes, we're so tired, we feel we can't go on. But God has always given us everything we need and never more than we can handle.

Our son has helped us become tough, and at the same time, tender. He sees life differently than

I do. Time has little meaning to him. Each day is new. A friend's touch, the smell of a flower, a new taste, a funny song—they all bring delight to his day. When I take the time to see life through his eyes, it's sweet and wonderful. God is very near to me then.

Shaun can't speak, so I watch his eyes and his hands as they express his mood, his desires, and his feelings. I have to slow down to understand him. Sometimes, his expressions are so quiet, I have to listen with my heart and try to feel what he feels. When I do, I think I see life a little clearer.

In Shaun's world, it's as if all the distractions have been taken away. What's left is what's truly real.

This experience has been the most difficult trial and yet the deepest pleasure of my life, and perhaps with it I've been given a glimpse into the heart of God.

Their process has obviously refined them. I hope it encourages you to allow your circumstances to refine you as well.

10. Stop looking back and wishing.

Whatever the problem, whatever the crisis, it's natural to look back to the way things used to be, to wish things hadn't changed. A little of that is to be expected. But too much of it keeps us from moving on to change our circumstances for the better.

Dwelling on the "what-ifs" does nothing to help us. Instead, it leaves us paralyzed. You may have done nothing at all to deserve the problems you face. As I've told my boys so many times, life isn't always fair, and unfortunately, we have to get used to that. The typical response is "But you just don't understand my issues and the injustice that's been done to me."

For all the mental powers we're supposed to have, when it comes to living life, we pretty much have one-track minds. We can focus on the future, or we can keep rerunning the old messages of the past. You can't change yesterday, Mom. But you can determine what you'll do tomorrow. It isn't easy, but it's possible. You may not have made the bad things happen to you, but today, you can begin making good things happen. Just stop looking back and wishing it had been different. Instead, look forward and begin planning how to make your desires for yourself and your family come true. *You can do it.*

If you find your mind dwelling on the past, review these points to get back on track and moving forward:

- Identify your real distractions.
- Release all anger in a healthy and productive way.
- Refuse to have a pity party.
- Think God is greater.
- Ask God to send His angels to help you
  (see Psalm 34:7).
- Learn, rehearse, and speak the truth.

- Remember that you can't change others, but you can change yourself and your responses.
- Remind yourself that life isn't necessarily fair.
- Choose to reverse your unhelpful attitudes and behaviors.
- Enjoy your newfound productivity!

CHAPTER 14

MEASURING YOUR ETERNAL MARK AS A MOM

A CERTAIN WALL IN OUR home was very precious to us as the boys grew because it was their growth chart. We never painted it in the 20 years we lived there. When we moved from that memorable house, a friend actually cut the Sheetrock around that chart and had it framed so we could keep it forever.

The boys always backed up to that wall over the years to be measured and see how they were growing. The wall was their standard. It was their measuring stick to determine how much progress they'd made since the last measurement. They were anxious to know, "How am I doing? How do I measure up?"

On the wall in our current home, the grandchildren love

to back up to this framed memento and observe their growth while comparing themselves to their dads' growth and the uncles' growth too.

Do you ever wonder how you measure up, how effective your mothering is?

One day Stu and I were sitting in a little restaurant in Chicago. "I'll bet that lady is a great mom," Stu said of our waitress. Here was a server who was in touch with her customers. She didn't just go through the motions; she was engaging. She really looked at people, and she talked *to* them, not *at* them. She really listened and interacted. She had a bright, winning way that was contagious. And she made people feel important. What a profile for an incredible mom, a mom who is sure to leave a positive, eternal mark. She just looked as though she measured up. We even told her we had her pegged as being a good mom and having some very lucky kids.

Do you wish there were a wall you could back up to so you could see how much you've grown, how you compare with the standards you've set? If I could make a measuring wall for you, I would pencil in some of the standards that make up the rest of this chapter. "Grow toward these," I'd encourage.

1. Am I creating a *positive* environment?

Is it so inviting at your house that the kids ask to bring their friends home? Is there a positive attitude in the air? Do they see you as someone who is on their side, someone who is interested in their day, their activities, and their needs, or do they see you as the resident grouch? Are you in their faces with stifling complaints?

If we want our kids to express happy hearts, it has to begin with us, providing a mirror of what we want them to reflect. It has to be caught by us before it can be taught through our reflection. And if we can instill positive attitudes in them, positive actions will result.

It has become a natural part of our culture to be sarcastic, to be patronizing, to be a complainer. But when we fall into that habit, it affects our whole attitude, and soon we feel that things are bad and unfair and that we deserve better. People with absolutely wonderful lives can become frustrated and depressed just because the trend of negative attitudes has taken hold of them.

What kind of atmosphere are you creating in your home? Are you capitalizing on the joys of family life and minimizing the hard things? There may be a lot you could get discouraged about, but what good would that do you? It may not be natural for you, but begin to count your blessings. Focus on the good. And when your kids do the same thing, reinforce it.

At our house, I often thanked the boys for saying thank you. That's positive reinforcement, a "thank you for saying thank you."

Finding nice things to say needs to be a forever rule. At dinner, especially, make it a time to enjoy one another, not to gripe and complain or to be distracted with electronic devices. Just as with praise and criticism, you need ten positive statements to balance out every negative statement.

When our boys started complaining (and of course that will happen in every home), I would sing a little song, "Oh, be thankful for the good things that you've got."[1] The end of that verse continued to instruct them and remind them of why and what their response should be. The guys have heard that from me more than they prefer, and so they anticipate my response. They say, "Don't tell me, I know—be thankful for the good things that you've got." Now as adults, they will occasionally sing that out loud, and we all smile.

That's right. They got it, and it is working.

Mom, I encourage you to give attention to spotting the traps of negative thinking in your house and to steer your children away from them. As a result, your family will more likely enjoy

- thankfulness instead of grumbling,
- confidence rather than doubts,
- peace rather than conflicts,
- trust rather than suspicion,
- certainty instead of apprehension,
- rest instead of restlessness,
- security instead of fear,
- freedom rather than bondage, and much more.

2. Am I creating an environment that's *motivational*?

In a letter from college, Blake was expressing his appreciation for the motivation he received at home. It worked for him, and he sees it working in others, as well.

As I've had the chance to work with a few specific freshmen on the floor this year, I've seen that the key is showing love and letting them see that you care about them and trust them as important individuals. That's enough to turn the most introverted or arrogant around into a smiling guy who wants to be around you.

It works at home, too, as you love your children and let them see how much you care. Sacrificing your time, energy, and talent for them speaks loudly. Kids usually grow up to be like their parents, whether they want to or not, because they live out what they've seen modeled. What are you modeling for your kids? Are you that quiet, steady, supportive influence that calms the storms and makes your kids feel important?

Part of creating this motivational environment requires keeping a careful watch on how much your children are "zombied out" on technology. That will mean monitoring how often and how continuously they use technology, as well as exactly what they are being exposed to. Overuse of these sophisticated babysitters can lead to shallow thinking and keep these kids from pursuing creative or right thinking.

A Pew Internet survey of nearly 2,500 teachers finds that 87 percent believe new technologies are creating an "'easily distracted generation with short attention spans' and 64% say today's digital technologies 'do more to distract students than to help them academically.'"[2] Not only that, it's hard for your children to feel positively motivated if they spend too much time on social media.

According to a 2017 Royal Society of Mental Health survey, Instagram is particularly unhealthy and is associated with high levels of anxiety, depression, bullying, and the "fear of missing out," as well as a negative impact on sleep and body image.[3]

That doesn't sound motivational to me! Do your research here, Mom, so you can create a motivational environment.

3. Am I creating an environment where we really *communicate*?

Communication is more than just being there when they want to talk. Listening is crucial, and your kids need to know you'll listen—really listen—when they have hard things they need to discuss.

But with teenagers, you're probably going to have to stimulate the conversation. It's in those unplanned, informal times that they're most likely to open up on the difficult subjects. You have to be initiating those times, however. After all, if both of you aren't comfortable talking casually, where will they find the setting to bring up that hard-to-discuss topic? You have to have a track record with them to make them feel secure in expressing their fears, doubts, and disappointments. And just making sure you're available to allow this to happen is essential.

In the process of all this communicating, you're able to have a finger on the pulse of your family. You're able to know where each is headed and when one might be drifting off course.

By knowing where the hurts lie and the concerns rest, you'll know why a need must be met *now*. You'll be alerted to step in and take action in the most appropriate way.

Leave notes, if necessary, to communicate plans for the day, expectations, and appointments. Children just naturally develop their own daily agendas if you don't remind them of duties or expectations. You can eliminate a lot of "Oh, Mom" statements if you communicate so your kids can plan your schedule into theirs.

4. Am I creating an environment that's *safe*?

We're usually pretty good about explaining boundaries when our kids are little: Stay away from the street, don't touch the hot stove, don't speak to strangers.

But as the kids grow older, we sometimes assume they'll know things by osmosis. The result is that they cross lines they didn't realize existed. Then it's confusing to understand why they deserve discipline or other unpleasant consequences for their actions. Growing up becomes confusing at times like that.

Drawing obvious lines and explaining expectations is essential. By stating clear lane lines and boundaries, you also provide comfort zones for your children. As you spell out scenarios of what to expect, they get a clear picture of how and why to make specific choices along the way. Too many kids don't have this help, and then they get in trouble.

Then as long as they stay within the boundaries, they know they're okay with you and their environment feels safe. If they cross the lines, they understand why they're being disciplined or left to suffer the consequences for what they've done. Those lines might relate to homework, dating, household chores, language, curfews, friends, and so on. Boundaries may also help protect your child from becoming a victim of sexual abuse that could negatively affect his or her life forever.

I tried to put messages I wanted our guys to remember into jingles or sayings that hopefully embedded themselves in their subconscious minds. One such reminder was of three things that cause teenagers trouble when they drive: food, friends, and music. One of the guys hopped in his car one evening, cranked up the music, and started backing out of the garage. He left a crease in the entire length of his dad's pickup and crunched the fender of his car before realizing what was happening.

Twenty minutes after the mishap when he bashfully came in to report it, I asked, "Couldn't you hear the metal scraping?"

"No, I had my music turned up," he responded.

"Didn't you feel some resistance as you accelerated?"

"Yeah, but I thought it was a shrub or something."

"But we don't have any shrubs growing in the middle of our driveway!"

The problem wasn't just that he couldn't hear the noise;

he was so attuned to the music that he wasn't aware of what was happening around him.

He didn't recall my warnings that time. But he found out they were valid. He understood he had crossed a boundary and would be suffering the consequences as a result.

So set out the lane lines, Mom. Give them a fresh coat of paint every once in a while so your kids don't forget where they run. As you do, you'll be creating a safe environment for everyone.

5. What about me? Is my life *balanced*?

Are you taking care of yourself? After all, how can you care for others if you haven't taken care of yourself? Keeping healthy requires a continual balancing act. But you owe it to yourself and your kids to be in good shape so you'll be ready to assist them when needed.

Make sure you allow yourself breaks—a few breaths of fresh air, a diversion from time to time, maybe a change of scenery. Recharge your batteries. Every mom should build into her schedule something to look forward to each day. It doesn't have to be a big thing. Maybe it's a promise to yourself to enjoy a long, hot bath. Maybe a half hour with a good book. Maybe a drive all alone.

If you have a physical or emotional problem, find help. Zero in on the causes, and find solutions.

Your unattended wounds may be affecting more than just you. Their influence may be wounding family members as well. So don't feel guilty about taking care of yourself so you can really take care of those you love.

Accept yourself. Everyone has strengths and weaknesses. Learn to accept yourself in spite of your weaknesses. When you do, you'll probably find you're becoming more accepting of others as well—most importantly, your husband and kids. And what an essential step that is in being a good mom.

Give yourself away. It takes a great investment of yourself in the lives of your children to be a truly incredible mom. Your involvement in your children's lives and activities will speak volumes to your kids and leave an indelible imprint— an eternal mark—on their hearts.

Too many moms have given up that involvement and attention. As their focus has shifted, families have suffered, and so has society.

So live a balanced life. Make time for yourself. But don't be distracted. Approach motherhood with a passion.

6. Am I creating an environment that's *gracious?*

Has experience caused your family to expect kindness and understanding from you or complaints and grumblings? Are you flexible or rigid?

If you've planned a family dinner and for various reasons no one shows up, do you make assumptions and attack the offenders, or can you withhold judgment and give each person room for presenting legitimate excuses?

When the children are little, are you willing to let your child and his friends build forts in your living room that stay built all day? That generosity may be remembered for a lifetime.

Do you have a "yes face"? Charles Swindoll tells a story reported by Dr. Karl Menninger about the importance of yes faces.

During his days as president, Thomas Jefferson and a group of companions were traveling across the country on horseback. They came to a river that had left its banks because of a recent downpour. The swollen river had washed the bridge away. Each rider was forced to ford the river on horseback, fighting for his life against the rapid currents. Each rider was threatened with the very real possibility of death, which caused a traveler who was not part of their group to step aside and watch. After several had plunged in and made it to the other side, the stranger asked President Jefferson if he would carry him across the river. The president agreed without hesitation. The man climbed on, and shortly thereafter the two of them made it safely to the other side. As the stranger slid off the back of the horse onto dry ground, one in the group asked him, "Tell me, why did you select the president to ask this favor of?" The man was shocked, admitting he had no idea it was the president who had helped him. "All I know," he said, "is that on some of your faces was

written the answer 'No,' and on some of them was
the answer 'Yes.' His was a 'Yes' face."[4]

Do you have the kind of yes face that makes your kids
feel comfortable asking? Does your yes face say, "It's okay
to make mistakes; I'll still love you"? Do they feel as if you'll
really listen to their requests? Do they believe they're important enough that you'll react to their needs with flexibility?
Do you find yourself saying, "Sure, I can do that with or for
you," even though you really had other things planned?

Being gracious means making kids feel that it's okay and
they don't need to worry about it. Sometimes—more often
than we think—kids need for someone to be gracious to
them, especially when they don't deserve it. Come to think of
it, don't we all? In fact, that's the whole meaning of grace—
undeserved favor.

7. Am I being *diligent*?

Are you giving persistent, attentive care to your family?

A friend served cauliflower to her family one night when
her son's friend was over. The boy had never seen cauliflower.
At his house, his dad brings home a pizza or some other fast
food almost every night. It's nice that this dad takes the time
and spends the money to lighten his wife's load at dinner-
time, but is that really the caring thing to do for the family?
Is that the best choice or simply the easiest?

Well, how do you stand against the measuring wall? Is

your measurement looking good as you evaluate? Do you feel like a great mom?

Sometimes—no, frequently—you feel anything but great. The routine seems so predictable. The kids don't seem to notice your efforts. There's little time for yourself.

Don't give up, Mom. Don't feel as if you aren't measuring up. You're doing the most important thing in the world. You're mothering. Someday the kids will recognize your efforts, your sacrifices, your support. Then they'll begin to show their appreciation. It almost always happens.

Here's an example:

Dear Mom:

I wish I could spend Mother's Day with you, but I can't, so I am writing a letter and hope you will read it in Ann Landers' column.

Mom, I love you so much. There are so many things that I didn't understand when I was young, but I understand them now.

I didn't have any idea how hard you worked or what burdens you carried until I traveled that road myself.

I didn't know how rough it was when you were having trouble with Dad and us kids, but I know now.

I didn't realize how lonely you were until I was lonely.

I didn't realize how hurt you were until I was hurt the same way by my own children.

I didn't know how many times I could have made you happy by just saying, "I love you, Mom." But now I know because those are the words I long to hear from my own kids. Whoever said, "Life is the greatest teacher of all," knew what he was talking about.

When I was growing up, we had more than our share of battles. I remember how I thought you were too hard on me, because you insisted that I keep my room neat, turn off the TV and do my homework, hang up my clothes, do chores around the house and write thank-you notes right away.

You made me do a lot of things I didn't want to do. You said it was good for my character. I couldn't see the connection. I thought you were nuts. But now that I have kids of my own, I understand things a lot better. I am grateful that you didn't let me wear you down. Remembering your strength gives me strength to stand up to my own kids when they try to con me the way I tried to con you.

It seems like I found time for everything and everyone but you, Mom. It would have been easy to drop in for a cup of tea and a hug, but my friends came first. Would any of them have done for me what you did? I doubt it.

I remember the times you called on the phone and I was in a hurry to get off. It makes me ashamed. I remember, too, the times I could have included you when my little family had outings, but I didn't.

It took me all my life to learn what a mother is.
I guess it's impossible to know until you become a
mother yourself. Believe me, now I know how rough
you had it and how terrific you are. Millions of people
are going to read this column today and see themselves.
Some will feel uneasy, and that's OK, if they learn from
it. Time has a sneaky way of slipping away. We become
so involved in getting from one day to the next that
before we know it, the tomorrows are yesterdays. I hope
this letter gives you an idea of how much I admire and
respect you, Mom. You really are the greatest.[5]

You *are* the greatest, Mom! You understand value—not monetary value, but the kind that really counts. You understand the development of the heart and spirit. That's what has real lasting value. And that's where you need to invest the best of who you are—in the things that matter the most, so that the main thing will always remain the main thing.

It's true, Mom, you're incredible! You leave an eternal mark on your children. You are shaping your child's heart, spirit, and future good life. You have every reason to feel good about who you are and what you do. God bless you!

CHAPTER 15

ARE YOU A TEAM PLAYER?

EVER SEE A 1,000-PIECE puzzle assembled with only 500 pieces? Something's missing, like half the picture. Ever try to create a great dish from a recipe with missing or wrongly proportioned ingredients? It just doesn't come out right. Ask any new cook who didn't read the recipe carefully. Something's missing, and the final product tastes like it.

Our kids deserve the whole picture. They need all the parenting ingredients, namely a mom and a dad. The Master Designer wrote His parenting manual, the Bible, with the intention that each child should enjoy the influence of both a mother and a father. The completed puzzle shows the necessity of a masculine leader to ensure the growth of a strong family.

No book can address all the aspects of being a mother and a wife. In this book, I'm focusing on the eternal impact of mothering, and as a result, little has been said of fathers. But obviously, whatever impact a mother makes can only be made stronger by the additional impact of a father. After all, the best strength is combined strength.

Consider this from an issue of *Our Daily Bread*:

> In a horse-pulling contest at a county fair, the first place horse moved a sled weighing 4,500 pounds. The runner-up had pulled 4,000 pounds. The owners of the two horses wondered how much the animals could pull if they worked together. So they hitched them up and loaded the sled. To everyone's surprise, the horses were able to pull 12,000 pounds.[1]

Combined strength, synergism—doing more together than they could individually. More than that, they displayed strength combining the best of both individuals, filling in the shortcomings of each. In the movie *Rocky*, the hero comments on the relationship between himself and his very different girlfriend, Adrian: "She's got gaps, I got gaps, together we fill gaps."

What Rocky had discovered, for all his perceived ignorance, was really quite insightful. He had noted an abiding principle. He and Adrian were different. Even more basically, men and women are different. Yes, different. Equal, yes; same, no. And in that principle rests a key to balanced, successful parenting. When we learn, as men and women, to accept and even celebrate our differences, our marriages and homes will take on an atmosphere we have all dreamed of from the beginning. And, happily, our children will be more likely to grow up to become confident, secure, effective adults.

We're often tempted to look at our differences with our mates as frustrations instead of realizing the strength that can come from our diversity. We need one another. Our kids need us both. When we enjoy parenting as a team, we are most fulfilled, and our kids are the winners. "A three-fold cord is not quickly broken," says the Master Designer in Ecclesiastes 4:12. And a home with a healthy mom and a healthy dad wrapped around the living Lord is a home not easily broken. It's a home where the sons are "as grown-up plants" and the daughters become like pillars adorning a palace (Psalm 144:12, NASB).

British psychiatrist John Bowlby tells of a study by Main and Weston focusing on the importance of a child's bonding with both parents: "Children with a secure relationship to both parents were most confident and most competent; children who had a secure relationship to neither were least so; and those with a secure relationship to one parent but not to the other came in between."[2]

What are some of the differences between men and women that combine to make for the most effective parenting? My husband, Stu, pointed out some of them in his book *Tender Warrior*: "A woman is more delicate. She is the fine china, not the stoneware. She is a finely tuned sports car, not a '66 Chevy pickup with mud flaps. She is more fragile, more sensitive. She has a more precisely adjusted sensory ability, especially in terms of relationships. A woman is more alert to what is happening in her environment."[3]

This detail-oriented beauty is tender and gentle. A woman's verbal communication skills generally rise above her man's. Cyclical changes continually bring reminders of difference. The nurturing instinct causes her to believe, trust, and give.

Does God have an obvious sense of humor by literally developing opposite sides of the brain between teammates? We operate on different frequencies. We need a good translation. Our men have a task orientation that equips them to make necessary decisions. They are so logical: two plus two equals four, with no variations. "Men are like soldiers," writes author Joan Shapiro. "They have to do painful and dangerous things without question. As a result, they become numb to their feelings."[4]

Because of all this, a man is equipped to be our initiator, leader, provider, and protector. He takes risks for the family and operates with a big picture. How essential it is for us to get a grip on the definition of masculinity!

How good that we're different. And how effective we can be when we identify those differences to understand our teamwork better! The sooner we learn this, the more prepared we are to live comfortably together and enjoy being the complements to our incredibly different teammates that God intended us to be.

In light of the importance of that teamwork, I give you another avenue by which you can be a truly incredible mom—*love your husband*. Really love him. Study your man. Learn how he works. Adjust to him. Any good teammate would. Accept him, join hands, and "go for it" together. (Love dissolves a multitude of inadequacies.)

Another foundational principle is equally profound—*let him lead*. Here's what my husband wrote about this issue: "Ever seen an orchestra without a conductor? . . . A boat with no rudder? A compass without a needle? Pretty pathetic. Nothing works right."[5]

Dad was designed for the primary leadership role in the family. Help him win at it. Help him lead by setting him up to do so. Show respect for his ways. Gently provide him with bits of information, little nuances of family relationships that are more likely understood from where your gifts lie than from his. Demonstrate confidence in his leadership. Back away from taking the reins at every juncture where you differ.

Our nation is filled with dysfunctional homes powerfully influenced by women who seldom acknowledge the positive role of the father in the children's lives. Those same homes often witness a dad who shrivels, drops into a passive mode, and lets his leadership role go. And the dysfunction will show up in the next generation. Richard Strauss tells us,

When dad abdicates his position of authority in the home, mom usually assumes the role she was never intended to have. The unhappy combination of a disinterested father and an overbearing mother can drive children to run away from home, enter early and unwise marriages, or suffer emotional difficulties and personality deficiencies.

Dad must take the lead. . . .

A dominant wife and mother confuses the children. . . . If mothers and fathers have equal authority, the child does not know which one to obey. He will use one against the other to get his own way, and will soon lose respect for one or both parents. Studies have shown that children with conduct problems often have domineering, high-strung mothers. But if a child knows beyond all doubt that dad is the head of the house, that mom speaks for dad, and that dad's authority backs up what she says, he will be more apt to obey and will have more love and respect for both his parents.[6]

Competition between mates means dividing one's strength against another. It means overcoming your opponent. And it means there's a winner and a loser. That should have no place in a marriage. But when parenting is teamwork, and when you can help your partner succeed at parenting, everyone wins, especially your children.

Consider the words of Harvard psychiatrist Armand M. Nicholi II:

> Let me make an observation about the emotional health of a family. If any one factor influences the character development and emotional stability of an individual, it is the quality of the relationship he or she experiences as a child with both parents. . . . What has been shown to contribute most to the emotional development of the child is a close, warm, sustained and continuous relationship with BOTH parents.[7]

So be a team player and love your husband—really love him. Make him your priority. Accept him. Let him lead. And help him succeed as a father. You'll win. He'll win. And most of all, your children will win.

Finally, a word to the single mom.

Unfortunately, you're not part of a marriage team. And as much as you'd like to be, and despite your determination, you cannot be all things to your kids. Whether you have girls or boys, kids need a male role model in their lives. Look for influencers who can fill that void. As my younger brother, Bruce, never had a dad at home, God brought three men—all named Don—into his life as father figures.

The first was the husband of the woman who babysat Bruce while Mom was at work. This man had meager means, but he taught Bruce how to work, how to fix things, and how to have fun in life even without money. He modeled the love of God, and the unselfishness he showed was incredible. This couple took Bruce into their home for years and didn't receive any money for their unselfish love given. They didn't want it, and Mom didn't have it to give. It was a God thing.

The second Don was an uncle who took special interest in Bruce. Having lost his only child to death after three days of living, this Don took it upon himself to be Bruce's encourager. He honored him on all the special days. He listened. He even gave up smoking when young Bruce expressed to him his fear of losing him to cancer if he continued. It was a great relationship. (He gave me away in my wedding too.)

The third Don was a camp director at Pine Cove in Tyler, Texas, where Mom moved when Bruce was about eight. Mom moved all the way down there from her home in Washington State because she felt God had called her there, and it would be a healthy place for Bruce to grow up, with plenty of positive people to encourage him and nourish his soul. Others looked after him, but the camp director was extremely giving and helpful to Bruce.

These were three special influencers who helped fill the gap. If you're a single mom, look for the same kind of loving, selfless men to meet your children's needs.

There's another family dynamic we haven't covered, and that is when Mom becomes a stepmom to children and Dad becomes a stepdad to children. Life happens, and things come into our lives that weren't part of our original plan. Now you need to provide unselfish giving not only for your biological children but also for the new children under your wing. Showing favoritism is not going to work well, so everybody needs to develop lots of unselfishness in reaching out to meet the many needs of all these children. The challenge is very real, and all the parents need to find extra measures of grace as they do their best at making the children feel important, accepted, and cared for. The children need as much security as you can find in your hearts to give them.

Mom, your potential for blessing your children is incredible. When joined with your husband's potential, it's even more incredible. None of us can do it alone. And even together, we'll always be working with both strengths and weaknesses. But as we say at our house, "We'll never do things perfectly around here, but we will always do them together." I hope that becomes your commitment too.

CHAPTER 16

DO I HAVE TO LET GO?

WHILE IT'S OBVIOUSLY ESSENTIAL that we prepare our children to handle a complex world, once they reach adulthood we need to let them go. If we don't, our children can become emotionally shackled and unable to proceed into healthy adulthood. If a mom doesn't let go of her children, they are not free to give themselves to another. Letting go is totally necessary for a life of healthy relationships.

While this is a required final stage in the nurturing process, it doesn't mean it's easy for moms to do. The day after our youngest son's high-school graduation, he moved across the mountain for work and to live with his brother. Although I knew it was coming, I still wasn't ready. It happened so fast!

As I sat at my desk pondering the busy graduation festivities we had all enjoyed, tears started to flow. When Ryan returned home at the end of the summer, he was there only long enough to pack and move to Wheaton College in Illinois. From that day after graduation, he wouldn't be living at our home anymore, ever, except for vacation visits. My 24 years of nurturing children in our home were done—and it didn't feel very good.

One summer he went to Africa on a mission, and then he got married after college. As moms, we have lots to adjust to, and this is a big one.

It was hard when we drove away from our firstborn, Kent, as he went off to college. My husband and I both shed some tears. A couple of years later it was time for Blake to leave, and the same feelings filled our souls. At that time Ryan became the only child at home. And then when he left, the nurturing window seemed to slam shut.

I'm not usually at a loss for words, but this time was different. Many moms don't even want to talk about it if the subject surfaces. Our influential years of preparing our children and shaping their lives are over. Why would any of us want something so wonderful to come to a screeching halt? (Okay, some parents are quite glad it's over, but I didn't identify with that.)

There were no more boys, big or little, in my house. I couldn't ask them what they wanted for breakfast anymore. It was hard making and eating strawberry crepes without them. I thought of all those unique birthday cakes I made each year for my sons—that was over. The athletic practice and game schedules were no more. No more hosting their friends all the time and providing lots of food. No more clothes to buy. No more "Whatcha got to eat, Mom?" Even as I write this, I'm overcome with emotion.

I would no longer be filling double grocery carts—it was amazing how much they ate! The neighbor was counting my seven gallons of milk one day as I emptied my car: He obviously had too much time on his hands. Or there were the 20 loaves of bread on one shopping trip. No more double and triple batches of cookies to make. No more loud music, empty gas tanks, or asking them to clean up their rooms.

College graduations are in the past, the three weddings are over, and we have a bigger family with daughters-in-law Carolyn, Jami Lyn, and Jessica.

As a public act of letting go of my sons, I wrote a different "Apron Strings" poem for each bride and presented it to her at each of the wedding rehearsal dinners. Included in the gift of the framed poems were apron strings that matched the color scheme of each wedding. This was an emotional experience for me as I handed my sons over to their brides. If you would like to do the same thing one day, one of the poems is included at the end of this chapter as an example.

As we first let go of our children, there is sadness. But we have to learn to move on. Carol Kuykendall wrote, "Though some grieving is normal, I knew I faced a choice: I could continue to wallow in nostalgia and dwell on the past—or embrace the future."[1]

Yet letting go doesn't come naturally. Christian leaders are quick to say that parental interference is at the top of the list for causing troubled marriages. It's a common problem. As the primary nurturer in the home, a mom needs an extra measure of encouragement as these nurturing years come to an end. Drs. Henry Cloud and John Townsend have some helpful insights:

> This process of leaving mother emotionally is the final developmental step for the child, enabling him to make a full commitment to adulthood.
>
> The first separation from mother, a physical one, is called *weaning* in the Bible. The Hebrew word translated *wean* is a positive word that sometimes means "brought up" and "to deal bountifully, to reward, or to ripen." The child is taken off the breast when he has had enough of the good stuff of early dependency and is *ripe* for the next step.
>
> The second separation—leaving home—has been described as the wounding of mother, which every child eventually does. They abandon her, in the sense that they grow up and no longer *depend* on her as *mother*. This does not mean that they no longer love, adore, relate to, give to, or receive from mother. *The relationship is not over, but it is changing.* Mother is no longer *the* source.

A mother takes great satisfaction in being her child's source. She is his first source of life and nurturance. And then his source of wisdom, discipline, friendship, teaching, values, and many other virtues. It is a very satisfying and rewarding role for mom. . . .

The sad news for her is that the role is designed to end. She gives life, prepares her child for life, and then lets go of the life she has created.

The "letting go," as we've seen, is the hard part for the mom. The child's task is to inflict the wound of leaving—to "take" his life and run with it. The mother's role is to "take" the wound and contain it. She sheds the bittersweet tears of letting go and mourning the empty nest. She watches as an independent person emerges—the fruit of her nurture, discipline, and love. Joy and sadness are the combined themes of this wound. It is at once a happy and painful tearing away.

To the extent that a mother is able to allow this step to take place peacefully, things go well. She has to reclaim the values of separateness, difference, limits, and assume a stance against regression. . . . She should relish in this sad step, and that is a difficult thing to do. But as she does it, she can see the independence of her child not as a threat but actually as a symbol of her good work: He is now on his own.[2]

To sum this up, these psychologists say,

The parent gradually turns over the management of the child to the child. The parental role disappears. The axiom is this: *To the extent that a person is being parented, to that extent this person is still a child.* The person who is an adult, yet acts like a child, will encounter problems when jobs and relationships require adult behavior.[3]

All this "leaving stuff" is part of God's design. Ruth Myers helps us catch this concept. "I am one of Your spiritual masterpieces, created clean and clear as a flawless jewel . . . and . . . You are cutting and polishing me to receive and display more fully the beauty of Your glorious attributes!"[4] Letting go can be part of this beauty, even though we don't feel that way at first. It takes healthy maturity on our part to do this aspect of the nurturing process well.

We received a gift some time ago that demonstrated the principle of letting go. The elders of our church decided to give Stu and me a special gift for 20 years of service after starting Good Shepherd Community Church and being lead pastor for all that time. They enlisted several master craftsmen within our church to design and create a beautiful dining room table that extends to seat 20, along with 10 lovely upholstered chairs.

Every piece of wood was handpicked from trainloads of wood. The table and chairs were crafted over a long period of time. Utmost care was given to the handling of this superior Pennsylvania-cherry masterpiece with 46 carved claw feet. After laboring over it with love, one of the craftsmen excitedly delivered it to us. I asked him, "How do you feel about parting with this when it has become so much a part of you?"

Without hesitating, he spoke profoundly about the principle of letting go. "This has been designed and crafted for you. Its purpose is now being realized as you take and use it. I took pleasure preparing it for you, and I walk away with no regrets knowing the purpose is complete."

I still get goose bumps when I think of his words! They capture the heart of our mission to nurture: to let our children go. God lets us participate in raising His children. When His purpose is complete, we follow His wishes and let them go.

There are so many illustrations that help us identify with this act. For a woman, it's easy to think of the gestation period of the child she carries in her womb. For nine months, the baby is protected with lining and fluid to aid in safe development. It wouldn't be possible for the child to live or be without problems if he were born too soon. Timing is critical. At the end of nine months, it would be absurd for the mother to say, "I don't want this baby to be born yet; let's wait a few months." But think: Do we try to delay our children's leave-taking when it's time to let go?

What about the cut flowers we enjoy from the florist? Holding them causes them to wither. Before they were picked, they, too, had to go through a long process of nurturing. If the gardener hadn't studied the needs, prepared the soil, fertilized, watered, pruned, and picked off the dead parts, the flower's full beauty wouldn't have materialized. If the gardener had been selfish and not cut the flower, no one else would have enjoyed its beauty.

We can't keep fruit on the tree, ships in port, arrows in the quiver, runners in the blocks, or students in school. There is a time to let go.

Another facet of letting go is allowing your young person to fail so he or she can learn. If we take over for them and they don't have to suffer any consequences for their failures, sloppiness, mistakes, and poor choices, we simply teach them bad habits. There are many ways that parents do this. Go back to that Bible principle in Proverbs 22:6, "Train up a child in the way he should go; even when he is old he will not depart from it." Don't enable your children so "they don't have to suffer" or you'll keep them from growing up to be productive adults.

If your kids borrow money from you, it's only healthy that they have to pay it back. It's offensive if an older child borrows thousands of dollars because he irresponsibly ran up his credit card, and then instead of doing his duty and paying it back, he takes an elaborate trip. You shouldn't bail out your child because of his lack of diligence. If you do so, you're letting him off while also teaching him to overindulge, which is another distasteful trait you don't want for your child.

In this letting-go process, let's make sure we don't participate in giving our children a sense of entitlement. Let them learn the very important principle of having good work ethics. You teach them this during your hands-on years of nurturing, so please, let them do what you taught them.

If we don't want to let go of our children, we need to ask ourselves why. Do we want to hold on to them, to keep them from going on without us, because of our own egos and our own insecurity? Do we think that they can't actually do something without our help or our presence? To make matters worse, some parents feel the need to insult their children and make them feel guilty because they're moving on without them. If this happens, their children live their lives in handcuffs. Oh, Mama, please don't do this to your child!

You are probably saying, "Our hearts are breaking over this transition, and you're asking me to be cerebral?" I've been in the same condition, so let's hold each other's hands and do our best. There are some timeless truths in Genesis 2:24, Matthew 19:4-6, and Ephesians 5:31: namely, to leave and cleave. It's a biblical directive for us to enjoy God's ordained best for us. We can choose to live life God's way. He does know best.

Carol Kuykendall writes this about the challenge: "Letting go is a God-given responsibility, as important as love in the parent-child relationship. Without it, children cannot grow. With it, they gain the confidence and independence to seek and reach their potential in life."[5] She also says this: "Our children will not give up their childish ways unless they sever their bonds of dependency upon us. They cannot grow up in every way unless we withdraw our control from their lives to allow them to mature independently. . . . We have to let go and give them the freedom to learn for themselves and to allow them to fulfill God's purpose for their lives—not ours."[6]

We start the process of nurturing healthy independence as soon as our children are born. When the umbilical cord is cut, children must take an active role in gaining sustenance. They eventually learn to feed themselves, walk by themselves, and ride a bike. Can you imagine how tired you'd be if you never let go of that bicycle? Later, we let our children go off to school, and then wonder if they can make it without us.

I remember the day Kent got his driver's license. Both Kent and Blake drove away that day for the first time. I wondered if I were ready for this. Was I foolish for letting both boys go together? Would they return alive? (Their memorable parting words that day were "Hope to see you again," which we've all repeated many times as we remember that day.)

But the stakes get higher. They start dating and then go off to college. All of these preliminaries lead up to the grand finale. It's like setting the stage for the drama with all the props in place. Are we ready to open the curtain for the act of independent living to begin?

Preparing for this stage requires good skills on the mother's part. Drs. Cloud and Townsend say,

The good mother . . . refuses to tie her children to the nest and instead kicks them out. By "nest" here, we mean dependent behavior past the time when that behavior is appropriate. The good mother then is internalized as a structure within the child against his own regressive wishes to be taken care of when what he needs is to grow up. Then in later life, when the person wants to bail out of adult responsibilities, a voice inside says no.[7]

Mom's personal insecurities can get in the way of the child developing a healthy independence. Cloud and Townsend provide this illustration: "Jeri's mom used guilt to control her. When Jeri would do or plan things that took her away from Mom, the message was clear: 'You are destroying me by being independent.' A child cannot cope with the fact that she is hurting her mother."[8]

There are many firsts. That time we didn't get a babysitter because they were old enough now sticks in our minds. We had attended a banquet and given the boys careful instructions not to answer the door and to stay inside. Unbelievably, at about 10:00 p.m., we returned to find all three boys sitting in the middle of the road in front of our house, just waiting for us. How could this happen? Fortunately nobody got hurt, but this "first" didn't go all that well.

Then there was the first time we left our youngest home alone while we were away on a weekend speaking trip. I worried that he would not hear the alarm and get off to school on time. Should I call? I decided not to. Did he get up on time? No. Did he learn the lesson for the next time? Thank the Lord, yes, he did.

Sometimes the best teacher is experiencing a "safe" failure. Carol Kuykendall adds this: "In [the] infant stage, we show our love by protecting them. As they mature, however, we must change the way in which we show our love to them. Slowly and gently we must give up this protection and control and allow them to protect and control themselves."[9] We pray for "smarts" for them and for us.

Before we build our building, we'd best start with our foundation, as we've said before—that's a given. Equipping our children means preparing them to make the right kinds of decisions. To bring them to maturity means to make them ready, or ripe. Show them how to do things. Then watch while they try those things. Teach them life skills. Talk about viewpoints they might encounter. Present those scenarios of diverse situations so they are aware of consequences. Tell them what is important and why. Tell them what to expect so they are prepared. Teach them about the differences between men and women, as we've laid out earlier.

Leaving home after being fully prepared is like taking a final exam after having thoroughly studied. Because you have prepared, you can draw upon familiar facts. You have confidence to proceed because you are ready. It takes the tension away when you are equipped and enabled. Moms, we can enable our children to have the same confidence for independence. We feed their root systems. They know their roots are growing and strengthening. They believe they are prepared to live without us. And we know that we can live without them by our side.

Our children will soar when we set them up for it. I can't help but think of the setter on a volleyball team who puts that ball in the air, positioned for the spike. If the setter doesn't place that ball accurately, there can be no spike. The setter is the key player scouted by universities.

You are the setter. You are needed by your children to set them up in life. Maybe it doesn't feel good to have done so much "prework" only to hand them over to their marriage partners. But that is the whole goal of the setter—to make the set for the winning spike.

Giving your young adults freedom, letting them go after "the set," is a gift of love. Ingrid Trobisch says it this way:

> Watch over your daughter in prayer, and then let her go. One daughter may be more difficult to release than another. You, as a mature woman, know that when your beautiful child steps out to make dreams come true, the stars in her eyes won't solve all the problems that arise. Still, you let go because ultimately, you respect her. You love her enough to allow her to make her own mistakes, walk her own pathway, follow her own timetable.
>
> Because you respect yourself, you allow your daughter the freedom to not live up to your expectations. This is the best gift of all.[10]

Releasing Children to Their Mates

Sometimes we need to evaluate our release skills, especially when our children marry. We need to ask ourselves if we would like done to us what we are doing to our children or in-laws. If your perspective is fuzzy, stand back and think things through. To participate in your child's healthy marriage will require you to see a need for your own separateness. As you gain this wisdom, you enable your child to gain the perspective he or she needs to develop a strong bond with a spouse. James Osterhaus has these tips:

> Healthy couples are composed of people who have left their families of origin. We've already discussed the verse in Genesis 2 about leaving parents and cleaving to one's spouse. Jesus reiterated this point. Why is this important? "Leaving" is an emotional separation, not so much a physical one. When I'm too close to something or someone I can't maintain my perspective or see from different angles. I will tend to center on particular flaws or assets without seeing the whole picture. As I get distance, my perspective changes. I learn to see my parents for the good and bad they did in my life.
>
> My separateness allows me then to enter into a close bond with another. The paradox of a healthy marriage is that two separate, well-defined individuals can enter into a bond much more closely and fully, while still maintaining their individuality.[11]

One friend told me of her experience with her mother-in-law, which unfortunately is too common. Her mother-in-law is "in their face" constantly. She questions the way they spend money, wonders why my friend does this and that, dominates their time, and intimidates them about their decisions. She undermines their dreams and goals and insists on being in the middle of everything.

This mom calls continuously and doesn't allow them to establish a life of their own. She demands their attention and time. She wants to know everything and be a closer partner in the marriage than she should be. She undermines them when they're not living life up to her standard, and they feel chained to her. My friend summed up her feelings by saying that she wished her mother-in-law would "stay out." This mother-in-law is displaying a strong sense of insecurity: She can't let go.

Ephesians 4:1-3 is a good passage about release skills: "Walk in a manner worthy of the calling to which you have been called, with all humility and gentleness, with patience, bearing with one another in love, eager to maintain the unity of the Spirit in the bond of peace."

Picture getting your child ready for a honeymoon canoe trip (if that's really what your kids wanted). You actually carved this craft as a gift for your child and his or her spouse. You have labored over this canoe for years. You chose the best wood and designed quality throughout. You have even helped your child ahead of time to understand the principles of balance necessary to avoid capsizing. Before they leave, you check for leaks. The new spouse is ready in the canoe and waiting to embark upon the journey.

Your child puts one foot in, but then can't follow through with the other.

What's the problem? You won't let go of your child's hand. With one foot in that canoe, there's no way that child can comfortably put the other foot in, much less paddle away and feel good about being with his or her new mate.

Because they are literally being held back, the couple can't paddle together. Every effort to take off is impossible because there's no freedom from the giver. Despite all of the wonderful preparation you provided, they become discouraged. If you continue to hold on to your child, this new couple can't embark upon this well-planned trip. Frustration levels will remain high, and the couple will feel pressure to quit.

Moms, we want to help them off, don't we? We want to encourage them to feel good about building a strong marital union. We want to support the right decisions that develop healthy independence. We want to enable them to cling to each other and not feel gripped by our control. It's a tough scene when the "child's" attitudes and actions are held hostage by the emotional grip of a mom's insecurity. The generations ahead lose unless we choose to build for the future.

Even though we may feel broken for a time as our kids leave the nest and build their own, we need to embrace those emotions and move forward. Ingrid Trobisch says, "Wholeness out of brokenness means rediscovery of simple pleasures."[12] She goes on to speak of such pleasures as wind, rain, snowflakes, a hug, and the skin of a baby. "It is also letting go of places and people you cherish in order to move on. It is sifting through the important and separating the good from the essential. Wholeness out of brokenness means hard decisions and difficult tasks that only grief-work can help you finish. . . . Wholeness comes in affirming everything and every place I have been as well as what lies ahead."[13]

When we come to the point where we can give the next generation freedom to grow on their own, we set them up to possess the security they need. Paradoxically, after we've granted their freedom, they feel more ready to include us back into their lives. That is experiencing wholeness out of brokenness. And remember, this might actually take longer than you think it will.

Matthew 6:24 says, "No one can serve two masters, for either he will hate the one and love the other, or he will be devoted to the one and despise the other. You cannot serve God and money." Yet when our children become adults and marry, we might want to hang on to being in charge. The ultimate act of nurturing is letting go, allowing our precious children the freedom to experience the world on their own. We give them breathing room.

As I was writing this chapter, I happened to be at the beach home of a friend who had purchased an exotic plant. When Donna took the plant to the house, she forgot to remove the plastic that was wrapped tightly around the pot. She watered it carefully, but because of the plastic the plant couldn't breathe. It was so saturated with water that it was "drowning and smothering" all at once. The beautiful flowers turned brown, and many leaves fell off. Death seemed certain.

After removing the plastic and letting the plant dry out, I removed the dead leaves and flowers. New leaves sprouted. It was exciting to see that there was still some life left. It looked as if it were going to make it. Had that plastic not come off, there would have been no hope. Donna came close to losing her plant because she hung on to a piece of plastic. This is a picture of the "letting go" principle.

When Mom takes off that stifling emotional plastic, she gives her child the space he or she needs. The child gets to experience renewed health. If Mom doesn't take off the plastic, she will eventually "suffocate" or emotionally harm her child.

As each of my sons prepared for their weddings, I knew I had to give them wholeheartedly to their new wives. I needed my guys to know that these ladies were to be the number one lady in their lives now, and that I was relinquishing my "rights." As mentioned earlier, writing the "Apron Strings" poems was a way for me to express my blessing of their journey together and of my "letting go." It wasn't easy, but it was the right thing to do. I cried as I wrote these poems, because these boys of mine were oh so precious.

To encourage you to do the same difficult task of letting go, I'll share the message my first daughter-in-law sent me later on.

You are the other mother that I received
the day I wed your son.
And I just want to say thank you,
        Mom,
for the loving things you've done.
You've made me feel extra special
as first daughter among the ranks
You've given me a gracious man
with whom I share my life.
You are his godly mother and
I his blessed wife.
You used to pat his little head,
And now I hold his hand.
You raised in love a little boy,
and then gave to me the man.
Thanks for such great gifts.

JAMI LYN

As hard as it is to launch your child into the world, the fruit is so good. When you let go, you're also passing your legacy to your children. Don't miss the blessings of letting your children leave the nest.

APRON STRINGS #1 FOR JAMI LYN
These apron strings I give you
from winding 'round my heart,
entwined around my little boy
And now they're cut apart.

I give them to you, Jami Lyn,
Blake's yours to have and hold;
I promise there are no strings
       attached
So your love indeed unfolds.

That place of being number one
I pass to you, sweet girl.
Although he's special to this mom,
His wife now makes life swirl.

You know you've got a winner
In this champion Blaker.
We feel he's chosen of the like kind
To please our great Maker.

We've prayed for you this man to take,
Your vows till death do part.
Commitment to each other speaks
of how you are so smart.

Now when I cut these strings away
To replace this cord of love,
I wrapped my heart around you both
Till God calls me from above.

We can't overlook the future
Weber generations to come,

Those little children announcing,
"Mommy, Mommy, you're awesome."

Jami Lyn, we do accept you
Into our big family.
May we seek the God of heaven
To live each day eternally!

I love you, Jami Lyn.
MOM WEBER

Conclusion

This subject of mothering is serious business. Mom, you have the opportunity to help your children develop healthy, long-term mind-sets and find purpose in life.

I hope that when you set this book down, it will be with a deep passion to embolden your children to be all that they can be. Mom, your efforts leave an eternal mark on your child and can help even the average kid be great.

And remember, successful mothers never give up. Many stand in awe of people who withstand unbelievable hardship and proceed with strength while completing important missions. Mom, you will overcome numerous difficulties as you continue to influence your child. As you press on to give your children the strength of heart to become all God has meant them to be, I place a wreath of honor on the door of your heart. God bless you now and forever.

The ball is now in your court. You can choose to maximize

your role and use your life to influence the next generation. My husband, Stu, has frequently quoted G. K. Chesterton, who said, "The object of opening the mind, as of opening the mouth, is to shut it again on something solid."[14] May you close your mind on that which is solid, and enjoy the fruits thereof. Blessings on you in your pursuit.

HOW DOES GOD FIT IN?

You may ask, "How does God fit into my mothering?" "He doesn't," someone may respond impatiently. "If you're going to talk more about God, I'm not reading any further."

I understand. Motherhood isn't the only thing that hasn't gotten much good press lately. To some, the words *Christian* and *hypocrite* have become almost synonymous. And Christianity is being portrayed by the media and Hollywood more and more as an enclave for small-minded, bigoted people. But there's another side to the story. So even if you feel as though God has no place in your life, will you bear with me for a moment or two?

Do you despise your wedding ring because someone

manufactures imitations made of brass or plastic? Have you thrown out your leather handbag because so many stores now sell "genuine imitation cowhide"? Do you refuse to drink fresh-squeezed orange juice because companies have perfected imitation fruit flavors?

It's no wonder the Christian community has so many charlatans. And it should be of little surprise to learn that there are hypocrites in every church in every town in the world.

It has always been true that only the precious things are imitated—gold, pearls, gemstones, great paintings, and other things of high value. Who do you know in the imitation paper business or the imitation garbage business? People always imitate those things that are most precious. But you don't throw out your prized possessions because there are imitations around. Nor should we throw out the opportunity for a personal relationship with the God who created us because there are fakers in our midst.

The hypocrites coming out of churches should be no surprise. They've simply become aware of their obvious needs, and they're going somewhere to have them dealt with. If we used the same approach to hospitals that we use with churches, many people would never go near a doctor or a hospital again. "You say you make people well. Hah! I've been watching who passes through your doors, and they're *all* sick."

The truth is, despite all the charlatans, all the hypocrites, and all the glitzy fakers who beg for your money on TV or loudly condemn you on a street corner, there is a place for God in your life—a precious place. It's a place where you can find open arms even if you're "sick" with the stains of the world and sick of yourself.

Knowing there are plastic rings makes your wedding band no less valid or valuable. Knowing there are pseudo-Christians clamoring for attention makes my faith no less precious to me. It's a treasure I would like to share with you.

How does God fit in? He fits very well right at the core of my being.[1] There is little space in this book on motherhood to tell you all you might want to know about having a relationship with God. But that's the answer you need above all else.[2]

Long ago our God condemned evil and all it spawns. Then He turned to us in compassion and said, "You can't overcome sin, can you? It's part of you from infancy.[3] But I love you, so I'm going to provide an Overcomer for you—My Son.[4] He will resist evil. There won't be found in Him any sin at all.[5] And after He has proved it, I'll sacrifice His life in your place. He'll pay the price for your soul with His life's blood."[6]

Of course, that Overcomer's name is Jesus. And after Jesus was executed by being nailed to a wooden cross and then was buried hastily in a borrowed grave, God the Father brought Him back to life. He overcame evil and sin and even death.[7] The price He paid, He paid for you. He had no sin in His life to pay for. Everything He endured was for you. And all you have to do to receive this amazing gift is just to believe it.[8]

"For God so loved the world, that he gave his only Son, that whoever believes in him should not perish but have eternal life."[9]

"Whoever believes in the Son has eternal life; whoever does not obey the Son shall not see life, but the wrath of God remains on him."[10]

That's the choice set before you. And your answer to the question of whether you believe will dictate not only the life you live now, but your eternal destiny as well.

When God created us, He knew what we needed for the enjoyment of an abundant life.[11] He issued us a plan to follow in the Bible. To the extent we follow His guidelines, we'll be able to enjoy His intended peace and fulfillment.[12] To the extent we choose to go our own way, we'll be left to experience the consequences of our own selfish decisions.[13] The choice is ours.[14] How does God fit into your life?

When we speak of being a good parent, of being a nurturer and encourager, there's no better model than God Himself. Who loves like God? Who has sacrificed more than God? Who has provided for our future more than God?

He has given us life. He is the sustainer of life—He provides every breath we take.[15] He's the One who longs for our friendship with Him.

He's the One who will always sit with us through our pain, our sorrow, our fear. He's our comforter. He's the One who nudges us toward good things and warns us, through our conscience, away from evil things.

He's the One who is always forgiving, always faithful,

always waiting.[16] He enjoys our growth and aches with us over our pains. He is *for* us.[17]

He's the ideal Father, and He wants to enjoy a relationship with you. When you believe Him and let Him live through you, you'll find peace and fulfillment such as you never imagined.

Think for a moment about the perfect mother. What characteristics would describe her? Maybe humble, wise, content, generous, self-sacrificing, peaceful, gentle, loving. But wait a minute. How can that be? How can she be content and peaceful if she has been sacrificing, giving, and loving? What about her fulfillment? What about her rights?[18]

It only makes sense that if we're going to be happy, we have to make sure we're getting our needs and desires fulfilled, right? And if we're humble, self-sacrificing, and generous, someone's going to take advantage of us, right? No, not really.[19]

That's why we need God. The world around us tells us we have to look out for number one, demand our rights, and stand up for ourselves.[20] Then we'll be happy. The result has been people who are more and more self-centered and selfish and yet, at the same time, less satisfied and still unhappy.

God tells us to go just the opposite direction of what seems so logical. He says to think more of others than ourselves, to give ourselves away, and to be generous, forgiving, and loving.[21] He says that in being concerned for others, we'll find ourselves satisfied,[22] whereas in being concerned only for ourselves, we'll never be satisfied.

Doesn't your image of the perfect mother prove it? It's her humility you respect so highly. It's her generous, forgiving spirit that draws you to her.[23]

That's not logical to a world demanding its rights.[24] But it makes all the sense in the world to someone who stops and really thinks it through from God's perspective.[25] You see, real living is not a matter of how we experience this moment. If it were, we should all seek immediate self-gratification, live for the moment, and satisfy our appetites. Instead, it's a journey to be enjoyed all along the way, not just at this moment or just for the goal. The selfish road leads us to walk alone, pursuing all we can gather into our arms. The godly road leads us to walk with and care for others and to walk with God. In doing so, we find all the peace and fulfillment that others grab for in vain.[26]

Too many people live by the me-first philosophy. And though they see no relationship between it and the strengthening or weakening of their character, it has its destructive effects.[27]

A couple of years ago, we learned we had carpenter ants under our house. The house looked fine. So why bother about a few ants in the crawl space? Because they were eating away at the foundation of our home. Left unattended, they would have destroyed the beams and sills. Imagine ants actually being a physical danger to us! So it is with the me-first philosophy.

A friend I'll call Susie had always wanted children. Her husband, Pete, kept putting her off, saying they needed to wait until they were financially secure. After 17 years of marriage, Pete still wasn't ready for kids, he said. In fact, he lost interest in Susie and their marriage entirely and had an affair.

Interestingly, the woman he eventually left Susie for had two children of her own. Soon another was on the way—Pete's baby.

Now caught up in the excitement of a passionate relationship with Pete, the other woman began to feel hindered with the care of her two sons. She actually ended up giving away her sons for Pete. The grandparents took over by default because the children were otherwise abandoned.

Pete was out to satisfy himself first. After all, he deserved to find fulfillment. He never found it, I'm sure. But his pursuit was a costly one. It cost my friend Susie 17 years of marriage, betrayal, infidelity, no children, no family, no chance to have children. It cost the other woman her children, her self-respect, and her future with her family. And it certainly hurt the two sons who were discarded along the way. (Those boys ended up battling drug addictions—are we surprised?)

The foundation was eaten away, and when things came crashing down, the destruction was great.[28]

Selfishness never results in self-fulfillment, only frustration.[29]

When I was in my late 30s, I became very frustrated. I wasn't generating income. I didn't have a title other than Stu Weber's wife and Kent, Blake, and Ryan's mother. And I wasn't feeling very fulfilled by all the little things I managed to do for everybody else. Who was I, anyway?

Questioning my self-worth was quite natural, of course, as I compared myself to "whomever." Even though I knew in my heart that what I had been doing with my boys was right and best, as was being a supportive wife, at times I didn't feel the value behind it all. Had I made a big mistake "just doing the little things" that so many don't respect as important?

No, it was a matter of thinking right, of playing the right messages over and over in my mind. But how is that determined? Giving of oneself is next to the heart of God— something we learn when getting to know Him. And taking proper care of ourselves in the process is actually part of the genius in living a balanced life. God more than okays self-care;[30] it's self-obsession that is forbidden.

I worked at becoming creative with this large balancing "act." My emotional needs improved when I planned diversions from the routine. Even ensuring basic things like exercise and enough sleep enhanced that self-care I needed. Maintaining a strong marriage has always been a priority[31] while carefully listening to my Lord about who I was and what I was seeking.[32]

God reminds me of my worth to Him when I don't feel much appreciated.[33] He reminds me of the value of what I do when others look down on my role as "just" a mother.[34] He helps me see the goal out there in the future so I guard my steps more carefully today and tomorrow.[35]

His Word tells me He understands my sacrifices.[36] His presence assures me I'm not alone.[37] His example teaches me there are lasting rewards for my faithfulness that will far outshine running after selfish appetites.[38]

He is my example.[39] He's my friend.[40] He's my nurturer.[41] He's my light and salvation.[42] He's my hope.[43] He's my anchor in a storm.[44] He's my guide when I don't know where I'm headed.[45] He's my comforter.[46] He's my source of peace, contentment, and joy. He's everything.[47]

How does God fit in? He's essential.[48] Whether you've never stopped to even think much about God or you've been a Christian most of your life, let me encourage you—seek God. Don't just concede His existence or pay Him lip service. Don't just fill your life with busyness for God. But seek *Him*. Really stop and seek after a personal relationship with Him and let Him begin to comfort and direct you.

Finally, I would encourage you to seek a mentor. Find a Christian woman you can really talk to. Someone you can trust. Someone who wants to help you grow.

In *Mothering Upstream*, Virelle Kidder says, "A mother without a mentor is walking a lonely road. She needs an older woman who will be her encouragement, her coach, her confidant. If you don't have a mentor, pray to find one. If you are older and hear God speaking to you about being someone's mentor, please take time to listen."[49]

I well remember what a mentor meant to me when Stu was in the military and we were stationed in Germany. I was expecting our first child, I was thousands of miles from home, and I had no family or acquaintances nearby. We had been in Germany for only 30 days, and Stu was already on a mission many miles away when I realized I was miscarrying.

I knocked on the door of a woman in our building and asked for her help. What a blessing to have this new mentor friend by my side to instruct, encourage, and comfort me through the trauma. When I got pregnant again, this mother of three was by my side, sharing her hard-earned wisdom. We need our friends and the strength of God through it all.

Because mothering is like sowing seeds, you don't often see the fruit right away. It takes time to reap the reward. There are no guarantees, either. But if you do your best, relying on God for wisdom and strength, there's a good chance that your day to see wonderful fruit will come.

Fruits of mothering will override the difficult earlier times. But Mom, you must look beyond the immediate challenges and keep those future fruits in view. May I encourage you to look as much as 500 years into the future? You see, you not only have a tremendous positive influence on your children now, but you can also bless multiple generations yet to be born. How's that for a big job worthy of the best efforts you can give?

How does God fit into my mothering? Very, very well. And I hope He fits very well into your life and mothering too. He has brought me and my family to this point, and He will carry my children and grandchildren into the years ahead. Let Him do the same for you and those you love.

What in the World Does Mom Do All Day?

MY HUSBAND comes home and wants to know what I've done today. Where do we start to actually relay such extensive information? He's had a demanding day too, but somehow it's hard for him to relate to what it's been like at home. After all, this isn't a "real job."

Wait a minute! We moms all know better. Being a mom is a job with a capital *J*. We work our fingers to the bone, push our nerves to the edge, and use every skill possible to meet the demands of the day.

Just what does a mother do all day? Today's college student can't imagine. Numbers of women are baffled by what they'd do with "all that time" if they *had* to be home. Sometimes even Mom can't remember.

It's the little things that matter to our kids, the things that meet special needs, that say "I love you." But if our lives become too fragmented by competing demands, little things can begin to slip through the cracks and be lost. Do they really make a difference? You bet they do.

Maybe you should make a list. You might be surprised at all the differences you can make. How does this job description match your own?

- Nuance reader of concerns in your child's heart and spirit
- Initiator of life boundaries and administrator of consequences
- Baby feeder, changer, bather, rocker, burper, hugger
- Listener to crying and fussing and thousands of questions
- Picker-upper of food and debris cast on the floor
- Coordinator of the kids' athletic practices, games, doctor and dentist appointments, haircuts, kids' parties, and the like
- Problem solver, determiner of action, and the one who gives those needed talks
- The person who reminds children of their responsibilities
- Comforter, encourager, counselor
- Hygienist
- Expert linguist for interpreting the dialect of the two-year-old
- Trainer of babysitters
- Listener—for the husband as well as the children— about their day, their needs, their concerns, their aspirations
- Laundry queen and stain remover

- Grocery shopper for all those continuous needs
- Meal preparer
- Dishwasher
- Maid
- Dog walker, animal caretaker
- Researcher of best prices for everything
- File clerk
- Teacher of everything from how to chew food to how to drive a car
- Assistant on school projects (collecting bugs, building papier-mâché volcanoes, etc.)
- Questioner, prober to promote thinking
- Filter provider of media and Internet activity
- Homework helper
- Reader of thousands of children's books (over and over and over)
- Planner and hostess of children's birthday parties
- Planner and hostess of adult dinner parties
- Short-order cook for extra meals that budding athletes depend upon
- Learner of gluten-free cooking for certain kids, or dairy-free, sugar-free, etc.
- Anticipator of medical/psychological issues
- Manager of appliance repair and home maintenance
- Executioner of ants, roaches, wasps, bugs, mice, possibly moles
- Resident historian in charge of photo albums, baby books, and school record books

- Resident director of Internet research
- Mender of anything broken or undone
- Decorator
- Officer of the day, on call for any emergency at home or away
- Washer of the windows
- Replacer of batteries and light bulbs everywhere
- Food preservation expert
- Family secretary, confirming dinner reservations, travel accommodations
- Reconciler of bank statements
- Tax record keeper
- Correspondent to the sick
- Archivist for everything that "must" be kept
- Gardener
- Keeper and locater of birth certificates and other valuable documents
- Ironer of wrinkles
- Seeker of God, one who prays
- Fitness expert
- Front desk clerk to keep track of each family member's daily itinerary
- Cleaner of the oven, the drawers, the closets, the garage, the curtains, the bedding, the windows, even the walls
- Emergency medical technician and ambulance driver

What else do we do as moms? Well, among many other things, you may do the following:

- Regularly clip 10 fingernails and 10 toenails for each young child
- Prepare costumes for various activities
- Return library books
- Organize digital photos
- Choose, purchase, and wrap many gifts for all the family members and others all year—birthdays, Christmas, Father's Day, Mother's Day, weddings, showers, anniversaries, and other events
- Mail packages, buy stamps
- Drop off and pick up dry-cleaning
- Get tennis rackets restrung (at our house)
- Have pictures/art framed
- Haul everything that needs repair
- Keep up relationships with the neighbors
- Keep up with all the various relatives
- Attend recitals and many athletic events
- Attend school conferences
- Chauffeur everyone everywhere
- Figure out what your kids are thinking and why and how to direct them in the right direction
- Cover for a sick kid on his 4:00 a.m. paper route
- Comb/braid little girl's hair
- Help in the classroom for each kid
- Become a mandatory volunteer for every fund-raising drive
- Keep up on the news, be informed
- Participate in school committees or boards

- Act as a room mother, making things and organizing parties
- Chaperone field trips and special events
- Plan vacations
- Coordinate car pools
- Serve as a Scout leader, Awana leader, Sunday school teacher, or other
- Purchase most everything for the family
- Deliver forgotten lunches, forgotten homework, forgotten athletic gear
- Attend church, Bible studies, committee meetings, showers, weddings, choir practices, board meetings, potlucks, and neighborhood meetings just to "stay active and informed"
- Make bank deposits and withdrawals
- Get the mail, sort, pay the bills
- Keep the car clean
- Refinish furniture
- Save lives—sometimes figuratively, maybe literally
- Possibly hold down an employed job or be an employer
- Make copies of necessary papers
- Send thank-you notes to givers
- Honor everybody's interests
- Teach your children how to save money
- Use gracious tactics to motivate
- Communicate continually to avoid confusion and misunderstanding

As a hub in the home with your children, you

- Relay the pleasure of your acceptance of them and their importance
- Draw them near to all that is important
- Remind them of your support and love
- Oversee continual choices
- Hear the heartaches and steer hearts toward healing
- Refresh concerned spirits
- Help ease the pain along the way
- Reinforce good decisions
- Model God's principles for them to follow
- Present scenarios before trouble erupts
- Anticipate their every need
- Look for opportunities to help them shine and take action
- Make positive connections with your eyes, heart, and spirit
- Tie together loose ends
- Guide them to better choices
- Ease anxious feelings
- "Feel out" the situation at hand
- Help them find higher ground during difficulty
- Provide ongoing encouragement
- Demonstrate ways to make things happen
- Teach life skills continually
- Provide security with your presence
- Show interest in their world

- Referee battles
- Look for trouble spots
- Calm their fears
- Praise the diligent
- Give hands-on assistance
- Smooth the way
- Watch for danger/disasters (foresee) and protect
- Find the safe way for them
- Place careful boundaries
- Stop destructive choices
- Lead them into positive patterns
- Enact the smartest plan
- Offer an "I'm here for you" attitude
- Provide wisdom/direction
- Expend your energy with purpose
- Pursue positive progress always
- Intercede in prayer for moment-by-moment needs
- Give of yourself to others, whether it's deserved or not
- Communicate at a soul level
- Find missing pieces for everybody's "puzzle"

Practically, you will do this with your kids:

- Talk to, interact with, pursue them
- Have fun
- Give advice
- Share the rules
- Discipline

- Show pleasure over them
- Encourage their giftedness and interests
- Spend time with them
- Sacrifice for their needs
- Hold them physically
- Encourage friendships
- Make provision for things to happen

I think this lady needs a spa day out, don't you? In my favorite book, the Bible, in Proverbs 31:10, it says, "An excellent wife who can find? She is far more precious than jewels." She looks out for her family in many visible and tangible ways, and she just keeps working.

What in the world does a mom who shapes her children's hearts do all day? All of this—and much more.

Acknowledgments

I'M FULL OF GRATITUDE FOR MANY. My own mother, June Lininger, not only gave me life, but was also a forever cheerleader for me. She believed in me and encouraged me to try anything, which I did. Through much family trauma, she modeled a very strong faith in God to enable us to endure anything. She has recently passed away, so she will be viewing the life fruit of this work from heaven.

Getting to be a mom to Kent, Blake, and Ryan was and is a gift to me, as you observed in these pages. I strongly acknowledge each one, and my husband, Stu, who has shared life with me as parents to these young men God gave us.

Focus on the Family is definitely to be acknowledged in possessing insight to allow me to present this needed message. From Larry Weeden at first, whom I was privileged to work with years ago at Focus, to Steve Johnson, to Julie Holmquist, my editor, who has worked feverishly to craft this with expertise—I say a large thank-you to each of you Focus staff people. Many thanks also to Dante Miro and Debbie Smith in marketing, Sally Sue Dunn, the skilled cover artist, and, of course, the partners at Tyndale House Publishers for their vision to strengthen homes through publishing this book.

Many agreed to be interviewed and allowed their stories to be told here. A large group of ladies in my Bible study and elsewhere have been praying for many details of this project over several years.

The Lord God has put this together and happened to use many of us in making this happen. And I wish to acknowledge each reader for taking time to absorb the biblical principles presented in this book so you can enhance your influence as a mom. Really, I acknowledge your perseverance in pursuing this work. You moms are shaping the world through the hearts of your children. Bless you!

Notes

CHAPTER ONE: DO WELL-ADJUSTED KIDS JUST HAPPEN?

1. Natalie Walters, "Brothers Who Cofounded a $100 Million Company Say This Question Their Mom Asked Every Night at Dinner Is What Inspired Their Business," *Business Insider*, December 17, 2015, https://www.businessinsider.com/life-is-good-founders-say-this-question-inspired-their-business-2015-12.

2. Ibid.

3. Ibid.

4. Leigh Buchanan, "The Inside Story of How Life Is Good Became a $100 Million Company," *Inc.*, September 2, 2015, http://www.inc.com/leigh-buchanan/life-is-good-book-review.html.

5. Bureau of Labor Statistics, "Employment Characteristics of Families Summary," April 19, 2018, https://www.bls.gov/news.release/famee.nr0.htm.

6. Gloria Furman, *Missional Motherhood* (Wheaton, IL: Crossway, 2016), 130.

CHAPTER TWO: IS THERE LIGHT AT THE END OF THIS TUNNEL?

1. Louis M. Notkin, ed., *Mother: Tributes from the World's Great Literature* (New York: Samuel Curl, 1943), 117.

2. Mabel Bartlett Peyton and Sophia Baker, *Mothers, Makers of Men* (New York: Exposition Press, 1952), 92.

CHAPTER THREE: DID YOU SAY *JUST* A MOTHER?

1. Cheska Samaco, "To the Woman Who Is Proud to Be 'Just' a Housewife," March 14, 2016, https://thoughtcatalog.com/cheska-samaco/2016/03/to-the-woman-who-is-proud-to-be-just-a-housewife/.

2. Ann Landers, "Job Description for 'Just a Housewife,'" *Chicago Tribune*, July 23, 1988, http://www.chicagotribune.com/news/ct-xpm-1988-07-23 -8801170398-story.html.

3. Pam Nugent, "Security," PsychologyDictionary.org, April 7, 2013, https:// psychologydictionary.org/security/.

4. William C. Menninger, "The Criteria of Emotional Maturity," © 1966. Used with permission of the Menninger Foundation.

5. John Gottman with Joan DeClaire, *Raising an Emotionally Intelligent Child* (New York: Simon & Schuster, 1998), 20.

6. Maureen Healy, *Growing Happy Kids* (Deerfield Beach, FL: Health Communications, Inc., 2012), 43.

7. William Sears and Martha Sears, *The Discipline Book* (Boston: Little, Brown and Company, 1995), 12.

8. Paraphrased from Rick Taylor, *When Life Is Changed Forever* (Eugene, OR: Harvest House, 1993), 14–17.

CHAPTER FOUR: CAN WE REALLY MAKE A DIFFERENCE?

1. Ray Guarendi, *Back to the Family: How to Encourage Traditional Values in Complicated Times* (New York: Villard Books, 1990), 121–22.

2. Ibid.

3. Barbara Berger, quoted in Ellie Kahan, "20 Ways to Make Your Kid Feel Great," *Parents*, June 1990, 95.

4. Kahan, "20 Ways to Make Your Kid Feel Great."

5. Quoted in Anne Ortlund, *Children Are Wet Cement* (Lincoln, NE: iUniverse, 2002), 58.

CHAPTER FIVE: OH, THEY'LL TURN OUT ALL RIGHT . . . WON'T THEY?

1. Ann Landers, *Oregonian*, November 18, 1990.

2. Tori DeAngelis, "Web Pornography's Effect on Children," *Monitor* 38, no. 10 (November 2007): 50, http://www.apa.org/monitor/nov07/webporn .aspx.

3. Eliott C. McLaughlin, "Suspect Faces Felony Charge of Fatally 'Swatting' Man 1,400 Miles Away," CNN, January 4, 2018, https://www.cnn .com/2018/01/03/us/kansas-police-shooting-swatting/index.html.

4. Joan L. Luby et al., "Preschool Is a Sensitive Period for the Influence of Maternal Support on the Trajectory of Hippocampal Development," *Proceedings of the National Academy of Sciences of the United States of America* 113, no. 20 (May 17, 2016): 5742–47, http://www.pnas.org /content/113/20/5742.full.

5. Ibid.

6. Sarah Knapton, "Motherly Love Helps Children's Brains Grow Bigger, Scientists Find," *Telegraph*, April 26, 2016, http://www.telegraph.co.uk /good-news/2016/04/27/motherly-love-helps-childrens-brains-grow-bigger -scientists-find/.

CHAPTER SIX: WHAT IS NURTURING, ANYWAY?

1. Robert Lewis and William Hendricks, *Rocking the Roles* (Colorado Springs, CO: NavPress, 1998), 215–16.

2. John Markle, "Text of McCambridge Letter," *Arkansas Democrat*, April 18, 1989, 11A.

3. Jon Hamilton, "Orphans' Lonely Beginnings Reveal How Parents Shape a Child's Brain," National Public Radio Morning Edition, February 24, 2014, https://www.npr.org/sections/health-shots/2014/02/20/280237833 /orphans-lonely-beginnings-reveal-how-parents-shape-a-childs-brain.

4. V. J. Felitti et al., "Relationship of Childhood Abuse and Household Dysfunction to Many of the Leading Causes of Death in Adults, The Adverse Childhood Experiences (ACE) Study," *American Journal of Preventive Medicine* 14, no. 4 (1998): 245–58.

5. Gail Gross, "The Power of Parental Influence in Child Development," *Huffington Post*, August 12, 2016, http://www .huffingtonpost.com/entry/the-power-of-parental-influence-in-child -development_us_57a6a8b5e4b0c94bd3c9a60a.

6. Charles Raison, "Love Key to Brain Development in Children," *The Chart* (blog), March 12, 2012, http://thechart.blogs.cnn.com /2012/03/12/love-key-to-brain-development-in-children/.

CHAPTER SEVEN: THE NURTURING PROCESS, PART 1

1. Ian Harvey, "The Tree Where Isaac Newton Discovered Gravity Is Still Alive and Well Outside of His Childhood Home," The Vintage News, March 17, 2017, https://www.thevintagenews .com/2017/03/17/the-tree-where-isaac-newton-discovered-gravity-is-still -alive-and-well-outside-of-his-childhood-home/.

2. "Isaac Newton's Apple Tree," The National Trust, accessed January 17, 2018, https://www.nationaltrust.org.uk/woolsthorpe-manor/features/the-story-of -our-apple-tree-at-woolsthorpe-manor; Richard Keesing, "A Brief History of Isaac Newton's Apple Tree," University of York, accessed January 17, 2018, https://www.york.ac.uk/physics/about/newtonsappletree/.

3. Ingrid Trobisch with Marlee Alex, *Keeper of the Springs* (Sisters, OR: Multnomah, 1997), 47.

4. Ken Magid and Carole A. McKelvey, *High Risk: Children Without a Conscience* (Lakewood, CO: Bantam, 1989), 62.
5. "Cyber Bullying Statistics," GuardChild, accessed May 23, 2018, https://www.guardchild.com/cyber-bullying-statistics/.
6. Justin W. Patchin, "Millions of Students Skip School Each Year Because of Bullying," Cyberbullying Research Center, January 3, 2017, https://cyberbullying.org/millions-students-skip-school-year-bullying.
7. Laurel J. Felt and Michael B. Robb, "Technology Addiction: Concern, Controversy, and Finding Balance," Common Sense Media, May 2016.
8. Graham C. L. Davey, "Social Media, Loneliness, and Anxiety in Young People," *Psychology Today*, December 15, 2016; Igor Pantic, "Online Social Networking and Mental Health," *Cyberpsychology, Behavior and Social Networking*, October 1, 2014.
9. A Parent's Guide to Today's Technology (Colorado Springs, CO: Focus on the Family, 2018), 3.
10. Monica Anderson, "Parents, Teens and Digital Monitoring," Pew Research Center, January 7, 2016, http://www.pewinternet.org/2016/01/07/parents-teens-and-digital-monitoring/.

CHAPTER EIGHT: THE NURTURING PROCESS, PART 2

1. Linda Burton, Janet Dittmer, and Cheri Loveless, *What's a Smart Woman like You Doing at Home?*, 2nd ed. (Vienna, VA: Mothers At Home, 1992), 42.
2. Betty S. Bardige, *Talk to Me, Baby!* (Baltimore, MD: Paul H. Brookes Publishing Co., 2009).
3. Helen Raikes et al., "Mother-Child Book Reading in Low-Income Families: Correlates and Outcomes During the First Three Years of Life," *Child Development* 77, no. 4 (2006).
4. "Early Caregiving Experiences Have Long-Term Effects on Social Relationships, Achievement," ScienceDaily, December 18, 2014, https://www.sciencedaily.com/releases/2014/12/141218081330.htm.
5. K. Lee Raby et al., "The Enduring Predictive Significance of Early Maternal Sensitivity: Social and Academic Competence Through Age 32 Years," *Child Development* 86, no. 3 (May–June 2015): 695–708, doi:10.1111/cdev.12325.
6. Anne T. Henderson and Karen L. Mapp, "A New Wave of Evidence: The Impact of School, Family, and Community Connections on Student Achievement" (Austin, TX: Southwest Educational Development Laboratory, 2002).

7. The National PTA, "Building Successful Partnerships: A Guide for Developing Parent and Family Involvement Programs"(Bloomington, IN: National Educational Service, 2000), 11–12.

8. Erica Komisar, "Just Be There: Why Moms Should Stay with Children in Their Early Years," *New York Daily News*, May 14, 2017, http://www.nydailynews.com/opinion/moms-stay-children-early -years-article-1.3160717.

9. Ibid.

10. Robert Winston and Rebecca Chicot, "The Importance of Early Bonding on the Long-Term Mental Health and Resilience of Children," *London Journal of Primary Care* 8, no. 1 (2016): 12–14, doi: 10.1080/17571472 .2015.1133012.

11. Ibid.

12. Anne Morrow Lindbergh, *Gift from the Sea* (New York: Random House, 2011), 40–41.

CHAPTER NINE: HOW CAN THE SINGLE MOM DO IT?

1. US Census Bureau, "Table FG10. Family Groups: 2017."

2. US Census Bureau, "Table C2. Household Relationship and Living Arrangements of Children Under 18 Years, by Age and Sex: 2017."

3. Patricia Daniels Cornwell, *A Time for Remembering: The Ruth Bell Graham Story* (San Francisco: Harper & Row, 1983), 229.

CHAPTER TEN: WHAT IS QUALITY CHILD CARE?

1. Bureau of Labor Statistics Reports, "Women in the Labor Force: A Databook," US Department of Labor, November 2017, https://www.bls .gov/opub/reports/womens-databook/2017/home.htm.

2. John Bowlby, *Attachment,* vol. 1 of *Attachment and Loss*, 2nd ed. (New York: Basic Books, 1982), xxix.

3. Jay Belsky, "Infant Day Care: A Cause for Concern?" *Zero to Three* 6 (1986): 1–9.

4. Komisar, "Just Be There."

5. Ibid.

6. Susanna N. Visser et al., "Diagnostic Experiences of Children with Attention-Deficit/Hyperactivity Disorder," National Health Statistics Reports 81, US Centers for Disease Control and Prevention, September 3, 2015, https://www.cdc.gov/nchs/data/nhsr/nhsr081.pdf.

7. Komisar, "Just Be There."

8. NICHD Early Child Care Research Network, "Quantity of Child Care

and Problem Behavior" (paper presented at the meetings of the Society for Research in Child Development, Minneapolis, MN, April 19, 2001), 57.

9. Tamar Lewin, "3 New Studies Assess Effects of Child Care," *New York Times*, November 1, 2005.

10. Ibid.

11. Kathleen Maclay, "New Report Examines Effects Nationwide of Preschool on Kids' Development," *UC Berkeley News*, November 1, 2005, https://www.berkeley.edu/news/media/releases/2005/11/01_pre.shtml.

12. J. Conrad Schwarz, Robert G. Strickland, and George Krolick, "Infant Day Care: Behavioral Effects at Preschool Age," *Developmental Psychology* 10, no. 4 (1974): 502–6.

13. Ron Haskins, "Public School Aggression Among Children with Varying Day-Care Experience," *Child Development* 56, no. 3 (June 1985): 689–703.

14. Deborah Phillips and Gina Adams, "Child Care and Our Youngest Children," *The Future of Children* 11, no. 1 (March 2001): 34–51, doi: 10.2307/1602808.

15. Ibid.

CHAPTER ELEVEN: BUT WHAT ABOUT PERSONAL FULFILLMENT?

1. MattAndJoJang, "The Story Behind Paul McCartney's Song: 'Let It Be,'" *MattAndJojang's Blog*, May 3, 2009, https://mattandjojang.wordpress.com/2009/05/03/the-story-behind-paul-mccartneys-song-let-it-be/.

2. "Paul McCartney: I Wish I Could Spend More Time with My Mother," *Telegraph*, February 26, 2013, https://www.telegraph.co.uk/culture/music/the-beatles/9896636/Paul-McCartney-I-wish-I-could-spend-more-time-with-my-mother.html.

3. Brenda Sawyer, quoted in Elisabeth Elliot, "A Cheerful Word for Mothers at Home," *Elisabeth Elliot Newsletter* (July–August 1991): 2.

4. Mary Ann Froehlich, *What's a Smart Woman like You Doing in a Place like This?* (Brentwood, TN: Wolgemuth & Hyatt, 1989), 163.

5. Ibid., 24.

6. Barbara Bush, "Mrs. Bush's Commencement Address to the Wellesley College Class of 1990," Wellesley College, 1990, https://www.wellesley.edu/events/commencement/archives/1990commencement/commencementaddress.

7. Devan Cole and Veronica Stracqualursi, "Barbara Bush Honored as 'the First Lady of the Greatest Generation,'" CNN, April 23, 2018, https://www.cnn.com/2018/04/21/politics/barbara-bush-funeral/index.html.

CHAPTER TWELVE: WHAT DO YOU SAY TO THE WORKING MOM?

1. "Moms Lean In . . . or Not," National Public Radio, March 12, 2013, https://www.npr.org/2013/03/12/174106545/moms-lean-in-or-not.
2. Connie Marshner, *Can Motherhood Survive?* (Brentwood, TN: Wolgemuth & Hyatt, 1990), 2.
3. "Helen Hayes Regrets Time away from Her Family," *Orlando Sentinel,* July 5, 1992, http://articles.orlandosentinel.com/1992-07-05/news /9207050344_1_helen-hayes-macarthur-acting-career.
4. Hana Schank and Elizabeth Wallace, "When Women Choose Children over a Career," *Atlantic,* December 19, 2016, https://www.theatlantic.com /business/archive/2016/12/opting-out/500018/.
5. Ibid.
6. Ibid.

CHAPTER FOURTEEN: MEASURING YOUR ETERNAL MARK AS A MOM

1. Evie, "A Little Song of Joy for My Little Friends," Why Complain (Waco, TX: Word, 1978).
2. Kristen Purcell et al., "How Teens Do Research in the Digital World," Pew Research Center, November 1, 2012, http://www.pewinternet .org/2012/11/01/how-teens-do-research-in-the-digital-world/.
3. "Status of Mind: Social Media and Young People's Mental Health," Royal Society for Public Health, accessed May 25, 2018, https://www .rsph.org.uk/uploads/assets/uploaded/62be270a-a55f-4719 -ad668c2ec7a74c2a.pdf.
4. Charles R. Swindoll, *The Grace Awakening* (Nashville: W Publishing, 2003), 4.
5. Ann Landers, "A Mother's Day Letter by a Voice of Experience," *Chicago Tribune,* May 8, 1994, www.chicagotribune.com/news/ct-xpm-1994-05 -08-9405080395-story.html.

CHAPTER FIFTEEN: ARE YOU A TEAM PLAYER?

1. J. David Branon, "Sharing the Load," *Our Daily Bread,* June 1993, no. 3.
2. John Bowlby, *A Secure Base: Parent-Child Attachment and Healthy Human Development* (New York: Basic Books, 1988), 10.
3. Stu Weber, *Tender Warrior* (Colorado Springs, CO: Multnomah, 2006), 130.
4. Joan Shapiro, *Men: A Translation for Women* (New York: Dutton, 1992), 220.
5. Weber, *Tender Warrior,* 49.

6. Richard L. Strauss, *How to Raise Confident Children* (Grand Rapids, MI: Baker, 1984), 120, 131.
7. Armand M. Nicholi II, "The Fractured Family: Following It into the Future," *Christianity Today*, May 25, 1979, 12.

CHAPTER SIXTEEN: DO I HAVE TO LET GO?

1. Carol Kuykendall, "Celebrating the Empty Nest," *Christianity Today*, September 21, 2010, https://www.christianitytoday.com/biblestudies /articles/churchhomeleadership/celebratingemptynest.html.
2. Henry Cloud and John Townsend, *The Mom Factor* (Grand Rapids, MI: Zondervan, 1998), 196–97.
3. Ibid., 196.
4. Ruth Myers with Warren Myers, *31 Days of Praise* (Sisters, OR: Multnomah, 1994), 75.
5. Carol Kuykendall, *Learning to Let Go* (Grand Rapids, MI: Zondervan, 1996), 9.
6. Ibid., 37.
7. Cloud and Townsend, *The Mom Factor*, 96.
8. Ibid., 97.
9. Kuykendall, *Learning to Let Go*, 11.
10. Ingrid Trobisch with Marlee Alex, *Keeper of the Springs* (Sisters, OR: Multnomah, 1997), 56.
11. James Osterhaus, *Family Tales: Rewriting the Stories That Made You Who You Are* (Downers Grove, IL: InterVarsity, 1997), 1.
12. Trobisch with Alex, *Keeper of the Springs*, 75–76.
13. Ibid.
14. G. K. Chesterton, *The Autobiography of G.K. Chesterton* (San Francisco: Ignatius Press, 2014).

AFTERWORD: HOW DOES GOD FIT IN?

1. Psalm 139:1-18
2. James 2:5; Matthew 5:8; 2 Timothy 2:7
3. Psalm 51:3-5; Romans 7:17-21
4. John 3:16
5. Matthew 3:13-4:11
6. Romans 5:8-21
7. 1 Corinthians 15:3-28
8. John 1:12
9. John 3:16
10. John 3:36

11. John 10:10
12. Joshua 1:7
13. Galatians 6:7-8
14. Joshua 24:15
15. Acts 17:25
16. 1 John 1:9
17. Romans 8:31
18. James 4:10
19. 1 Corinthians 2:14; Philippians 2:2-11; 1 Corinthians 3:18-19
20. 2 Timothy 3:1-5
21. Matthew 5:39-48
22. John 12:24-26; Luke 17:33; Acts 20:35; Philippians 2:3-8
23. Proverbs 31:28
24. 2 Corinthians 4:4
25. 2 Corinthians 4:6
26. Philippians 4:7
27. Philippians 2:2-5; Proverbs 16:18; Proverbs 28:26
28. Philippians 3:19
29. Philippians 3:18-19
30. 1 Peter 3:3-4; 1 Corinthians 3:16
31. Titus 2:4-5
32. 1 Chronicles 28:9
33. Ephesians 2:10
34. Proverbs 31:10, 28
35. Hebrews 13:5; Psalm 23
36. Galatians 6:9
37. Hebrews 13:5
38. Proverbs 11:18
39. Psalm 26:3
40. John 15:15
41. Hebrews 13:21
42. Psalm 27:1
43. Psalm 39:7
44. Hebrews 6:19
45. Psalm 48:14
46. 2 Corinthians 1:3-7
47. Psalm 18:2
48. Colossians 1:17
49. Virelle Kidder, *Mothering Upstream* (Wheaton, IL: Victor, 1990), 32.

About the Author

LINDA WEBER is a best-selling author and speaker, and a dedicated wife, mother, and mother-in-law. She's also an active "gramma" to 10 grandchildren. While her children were young, she was a stay-at-home mom. In a different stage of life, Linda was named as a top salesperson in a large retail chain, even as a part-timer. Then she became a multimillion-dollar real estate broker/producer. Linda and her husband, Stu, were FamilyLife speakers for a season. Linda has been a pastor's wife for 40 years at a large church that she and Stu founded. She has done large-scale entertaining and has traveled throughout the country and world. She enjoys tennis, home decorating, cooking, and taking and keeping many photographic memories. She loves leading a Bible study group, and her love for God and His Word rules her life.

Linda Weber's contact:
PO Box 812
Troutdale, OR 97060
(Please include e-mail on any correspondence.)

Meet the rest of the family

Expert advice on parenting and marriage . . . spiritual growth . . . powerful personal stories . . .

Focus on the Family's collection of inspiring, practical resources can help your family grow closer to God—and each other—than ever before. Whichever format you need—video, audio, book, or e-book—we have something for you. Discover how to help your family thrive with books, DVDs, and more at **FocusOnTheFamily.com/resources**.

Inspiring Books to Guide Your Journey of Adoption

CP1361